MODERN WORLD NATIONS

MODERN WORLD NATIONS

Greece

Zoran Pavlović

Series Consulting Editor
Charles F. Gritzner
South Dakota State University

CHELSEA HOUSE
PUBLISHERS
An imprint of Infobase Publishing

Frontispiece: Flag of Greece

Cover: Greek houses and windmill, Santorini Island, Cyclades, Greece.

Greece

Copyright © 2006 by Infobase Publishing

All rights reserved. No part of this book may be reproduced or utilized in any form or by any means, electronic or mechanical, including photocopying, recording, or by any information storage or retrieval systems, without permission in writing from the publisher. For information contact:

Chelsea House
An imprint of Infobase Publishing
132 West 31st Street
New York NY 10001

Library of Congress Cataloging-in-Publication Data

Pavlovic, Zoran.
  Greece / Zoran Pavlovic.
    p. cm. — (Modern world nations)
  Includes bibliographical references and index.
  ISBN 0-7910-8797-2 (hard cover)
  1. Greece—Geography—Juvenile literature. I. Title. II. Series.
DF720.P38 2005
914.95—dc22   2005031779

Chelsea House books are available at special discounts when purchased in bulk quantities for businesses, associations, institutions, or sales promotions. Please call our Special Sales Department in New York at (212) 967-8800 or (800) 322-8755.

You can find Chelsea House on the World Wide Web at http://www.chelseahouse.com

Text and cover design by Takeshi Takahashi

Printed in the United States of America

Bang 21C 10 9 8 7 6 5 4 3 2 1

This book is printed on acid-free paper.

All links, web addresses, and Internet search terms were checked and verified to be correct at the time of publication. Because of the dynamic nature of the web, some addresses and links may have changed since publication and may no longer be valid.

Table of Contents

MODERN WORLD NATIONS

Greece

1

Introducing Greece

Atop the hill overlooking Athens, Greece's capital city, lies the Acropolis. This famous cultural relic is more than simply one of the country's best known archaeological monuments. It also serves as a majestic reminder of an era when Greek civilization dominated the known world. The influence of the ancient Greek culture reached from the Straight of Gibraltar to as far east as the Himalaya Mountains. Zeus and other gods from Greek mythology were well known throughout Europe, Africa, and Asia. Both warriors and merchants, with sword and gold, were spreading Greek knowledge, inventions, and philosophy. For their accomplishments in learning and the spread of their knowledge, the ancient Greeks were known by other cultures as the "people of the book."

Roots of many modern scientific disciplines, including geography, are found in ancient Greek civilization. Before what we recognize today as "geography" existed, Greeks were actively practicing the science.

Athens, pictured here from atop Lycabettus Hill, east of the city, is the capital of Greece and regarded by many as the birthplace of Western Civilization. The Acropolis, the center of ancient Athens's chief religious and municipal buildings, can be seen in the center of the photo.

(It was not until 200 B.C. that the Greek scholar Eratosthenes first used the word *geography*, meaning "writing about the earth".) These early people, tucked away in a distant corner of Europe, had long studied changes taking place on the earth's surface. They analyzed differences and similarities between places and wondered why certain things were happening in certain locations. In essence, they were interested in the importance of location and spatial patterns—the foundations of modern geographic thought. Fortunately for us, much of their early thoughts were preserved in manuscripts for thousands of years. In recent centuries, this information served as the foundation from which modern geography and most other sciences grew.

Today, we respect the works of Greek scholars such as Herodotus and Eratosthenes for their observations about the land and people. The same can be said for Greek observations on philosophy, physics, mathematics, and many other disciplines. One must not forget contributions from Plato and Aristotle, Archimedes, Pythagoras, and many others. These names are recognized in classrooms around the world. Most scholars give generous credit to the Greeks for their role in building the springboard that launched Western Civilization.

Greece then and now is not the same, however. Contemporary Greece is far from the world's leading civilization. It holds a place as a small nation-state in southeastern Europe, created through many years of cultural struggle. The gods of Mount Olympus are long gone. To most modern Greeks, soccer stars are much more important than the stars studied by the ancient cosmographers (who studied the cosmos, or universe). Winning European championships in soccer and basketball take precedence nowadays. The Greek world and culture are vastly changed from what they once were.

THEN AND NOW

Times and the Greek culture (way of life) have changed. What has not changed is the beauty of the Aegean Peninsula and surrounding islands; the area of the world that we now call the country of Greece. Mountains rising abruptly out of the sea, crystal clear waters of the Mediterranean, and hundreds of islands are postcard images of Greece. Quite often, however, postcard photographs are not accurate depictions. Their primary purpose is to portray idyllic pictures of foreign places. They show what the place should be like in our dreams, rather than what the place is like in reality.

In the case of Greece, postcards do not need Photoshop enhancement. Towering Mount Olympus, seawater the color of the most precious sapphires, the greenness of delicious olives, and the redness of wine are a Greek reality. Add to the natural splendor the hundreds of architectural and archaeological treasures the country offers and Greece is a place that everyone should visit at least once in their lifetime!

Most Greeks, of course, are extremely proud of their country; to them, it is much more than a tourist destination. They are proud that after many centuries of foreign domination, Greece is now an independent country. In this part of the world, peace is a relative term. Historically, war has broken out on many occasions in the region. Boundaries have changed many times, and there have been wide-scale human migrations resulting from political conflict. Greeks have suffered their share of hardships. Because of these historical circumstances, many Greeks have left their homeland. Today, people of Greek descent live in places throughout the world and number in the millions.

Sharp cultural contrasts are another factor that makes Greece such a wonderful country to study geographically. There is the ongoing transformation from a sleepy traditional rural and village agricultural way of life into a rapidly growing urban culture and modern lifestyle. The culture change occurring in countries such as Greece is, perhaps, what leads to the creation of a modern world nation. Tradition-bound folk culture is being replaced by a new type of popular cultural lifestyle marked by change. The rapid transformation of society from rural into urban often marks uneven progress. Later in this book, we will explore some of the major difficulties for Greece: the large gaps in economic growth among its different regions. These differences contribute significantly to other aspects of Greek lifestyle.

Greeks share their love of life and offer open hospitality. No matter what part of the country a person visits, he or she can always count on a warm greeting from local people. This is one of those traditional traits that hopefully will not disappear with expanding urban popular culture. Celebration of life—the need for good food, friendship, and strong family ties—are traits deeply entrenched in Greek culture.

This book is not intended to be a detailed, statistical, encyclopedic survey of Greece. Rather, it focuses on the main aspects of Greek culture—those things that make the country and its people unique. In order to fully understand Greek (or any other) culture, one must first understand its background.

The following chapter is devoted to the physical geography of the Aegean Peninsula and surrounding islands. The natural environment sets the stage on which cultural activities take place. Nature provides opportunities but can create obstacles. It is up to people, based on their culture, to adapt to, use, and modify the lands in which they live.

We will then move on to a brief survey of the country's historical geography. A prominent geographer, Erhard Rostlund, once noted that "the present is the fruit of the past and contains the seeds of the future." In essence, without looking to the past, it is difficult if not impossible to understand the present or gaze into the future. Current cultural geography is the result of historical development. Chapter 4 portrays Greek culture as it is today.

Economics and politics are two elements of culture that warrant our attention. Study of these disciplines is essential to the well-being of both humans and the countries in which they reside. They also provide a picture of day-to-day life of a country's people. Because of their importance, a chapter is devoted both to economic and to political geography. Finally, before concluding and projecting the future geography of Greece, you will be taken on a tour of the country's diverse regions.

You are now beginning a process of filling in your "mental map" of Greece, by learning about the country's geographic conditions and patterns. Individuals who possess a detailed mental map of a region can much easier imagine what places are like. Albert Einstein once noted that "Imagination is more important than knowledge." Imagination, after all, does not adhere to any boundaries. Are you ready to begin your imaginary journey of discovery to the fabled land of Greece?

CHAPTER

2

Physical Landscapes

G eography can be defined as the science involved in the study of "What is where, why there, and why care?" Whatever one studies—whether it is the physical or human features of the earth's surface—it becomes geographical the moment a spatial methodology (location) is used to explain certain phenomena. Geographers try to understand how places and the various features that make them unique are similar to or different from one another. They want to know why differences exist from place to place. The location of a place often provides clues to its unique physical and cultural development. These are the foundations of geographic study.

Culture is the way that humans adapt. That is, by using knowledge, tools, and skills, they are able to develop a way of life best suited to a particular location and environment. Knowing where people live can often tell us a great deal about their culture. For example, fertile soils accumulate in the immediate vicinity of certain volcanoes.

If agriculture is important to a culture, it will take advantage of this natural condition, and farming will be a major economic activity. With productive farming on the rich soils, the area also will experience a higher population density than other, less fertile, areas. Almost all early civilizations developed in areas that were well suited to agriculture, such as river valleys.

Greece is located on the southern tip of the Balkan Peninsula. In practical terms, the region is not really a peninsula. Rather, "Balkan" more correctly refers to the cultural region located in southeastern Europe southward from the Sava and Danube rivers. It includes countries of the former Yugoslavia (Slovenia, Croatia, Bosnia and Herzegovina, Serbia and Montenegro, and Macedonia), Bulgaria, Albania, and Greece. Some scholars include Romania and European Turkey in this group, as well.

Greek tribes moved into southeastern Europe as early as 2,000 B.C. There, they developed a thriving civilization in one of the most attractive corners of the Mediterranean. It was an area with a very pleasant climate, varied terrain consisting of mountains and fertile valleys, and seas with hundreds of islands scattered around the mainland. From this location at the southern tip of the Balkans and sandwiched between the Ionian and Aegean seas, the Greeks expanded to settle much of the rest of the Mediterranean realm. Greece, itself, remained the Mediterranean cultural center for many centuries. Because almost three-fourths of Greece is mountainous, the country has always looked outward. Often, this led to emigration (migration out of a country). It also helped turn the Greeks toward the sea.

Eventually, the center of cultural dominance and political power shifted from the eastern Mediterranean to northwestern Europe. Today, culturally, Greece remains somewhat outside mainstream European centers. The importance of location has changed, as has the spatial distribution of power.

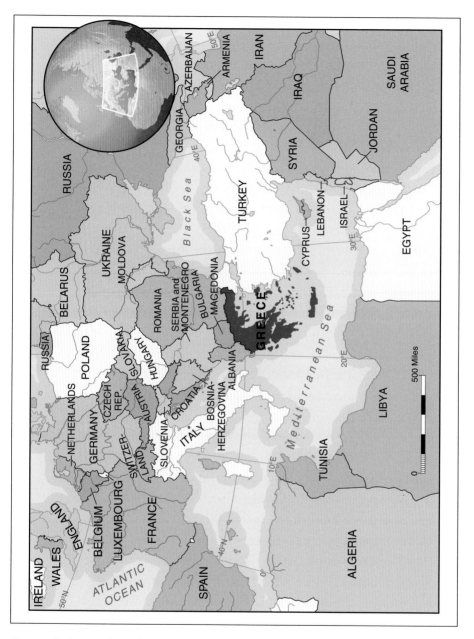

Greece is located on the southern end of the Balkan Peninsula, in south-eastern Europe. In addition to Greece, the nations of Slovenia, Croatia, Bosnia and Herzegovina, Serbia and Montenegro, Macedonia, Bulgaria, Albania, and sometimes Romania and European Turkey are recognized as part of this peninsula.

It was not until the twentieth century that Greece finally assumed its current geographic area and shape. In addition to the country's territory on the European mainland, there are numerous islands in the surrounding seas, including most of the islands in the Aegean Sea. Greece occupies an area of 51,146 square miles (131,468 square kilometers), making it about the size of Alabama or Louisiana. By European standards, it is a midsized country, but in global terms, it occupies a small area. Most of Greece lies roughly between 35 and 42 degrees north latitude. Athens is located at approximately the same latitude as San Francisco, St. Louis, or Washington, D.C.

THE LAND

As noted earlier, the topography of Greece is primarily made up of hills and mountains—both on the mainland and islands—the highest of which are located in the northern and western part of the country. Lowlands of any size are found only in the northeast, bordering Turkey and Bulgaria. Rugged terrain is the direct result of geological events spanning millions of years.

A look at a map of Europe reveals the general east-west and northwest-southeast direction of mountain ranges. The formation of southeastern Europe's mountains began about 60 million years ago, and the process continues today. Mountain building begins when the movement of tectonic plates causes them to collide. During this process, one tectonic plate slides beneath another, forcing it upward and creating mountains. This violent process often generates earthquakes and can also create volcanoes. These processes can be seen closer to home, in California.

Land conditions in Greece are the result of a collision between Europe and Africa—that is, the process in which the African tectonic plate is slowly pushing into the European plate. Although the clash of plates is less violent than in some other parts of the world, active volcanoes scattered throughout the Mediterranean serve as a reminder that it is still very much

With the exception of the northeastern portion of Greece, which is predominantly lowlands, the topography of the country consists primarily of mountains and hills. Greece is surrounded on three sides by water and includes approximately 2,000 islands in the Aegean, Ionian, and Mediterranean seas.

alive. On the Greek mainland, the only volcanic activity is found on the Peloponnesus Peninsula. The Greek islands, however, are home to some of the world's best known volcanoes. Location again proves to be important. The volcanoes are located in an area known as the Aegean Volcanic Arc of the eastern Mediterranean. It follows the subduction zone, or deep sea trench, formed where the African and European plates collide. This zone, just off the Greek coast, is also the deepest point in the Mediterranean Sea, with a depth of almost 15,000 feet (4,572 meters).

One of the volcanic islands, Santorini (also historically known as Thera), belongs to a famous group of volcanoes. It is still active and represents a potential danger to people living nearby. Its fame, though, dates to around 1,650 B.C., when a violent eruption and resulting tsunami (tidal wave) devastated early cultures in the eastern Mediterranean. The eruption was so strong that many hundreds of miles away, in Asia and Africa, people felt its effects and recorded the event in their historical annals. Many scholars even believe the story of the mythical island of Atlantis, to which the philosopher Plato famously referred in his writings, was in fact a description of the Santorini eruption. Plato noted that a well-developed civilization existed on the island of Atlantis, but disappeared when the island vanished beneath the sea because of violent natural forces. Even if not true, the legend of Atlantis is a fascinating story that has puzzled generations of scholars and laypeople alike.

About 2,000 islands scattered about the Aegean, Ionian, and Mediterranean seas belong to Greece. They vary in size from little more than small rocks protruding from the water to Greece's largest island, Crete. Islands generally are rugged and quite dry, without major streams. Most of their settlements are oriented toward the sea. The Greek coastline measures almost 8,500 miles (13,676 kilometers) in length, which for such a small country is impressive. One might imagine that at one point, Greece, like Norway, had many alpine-type glaciers sliding into the sea and sculpting spectacular valleys. That was not the case, however. During the Ice Age, Greece was too far south to have major glaciers. Rather, its rugged coast was the result of tectonics (earth-building forces). The Peloponnesus Peninsula, which accounts for a large portion of the mainland, serves as a good example of how these forces shaped the country. The peninsula is connected to the mainland by a thin sliver of land that today is severed by the Corinth Canal (which technically makes Peloponnesus an island).

Greek topography is dominated by mountains separated by short valleys. In some places, mountains rise spectacularly straight out of the sea. Elsewhere, natural forces created small plains or valleys, especially in areas near the coast. Coastal plains were utilized from the beginning of the human occupation of Greece. Through time, a number of large settlements, including the capital and the largest city, Athens, were established on flat, low-lying, coastal lands. Inland, the Pindus Mountains are the country's most significant mountain range. As a southern extension of the Dinaric Alps, the Pindus spread from Macedonia through the center of Greece, all the way to its southern margin. Famous Mount Olympus, with all its mystical spirits, is the country's highest point, reaching an elevation of 9,570 feet (2,917 meters).

CLIMATE

Climate is a long-term average of weather conditions, whereas weather is the current atmospheric condition we talk about on a daily basis. Except for higher elevations, the climate in Greece is predominantly Mediterranean. This mild and pleasant climate takes its name from the conditions that surround much of the European Mediterranean Basin. Major characteristics of this climate type are long, warm summers and mild winters. This climate, regarded by many people to be the world's most pleasant, also occurs in southern coastal California. Most precipitation falls during the winter months,

The nation's principal mountain range is the Pindus (Píndhos in Greek), which run south from Macedonia and Albania to central Greece. A southern extension of the Dinaric Alps, the Pindus divide the Greek provinces of Thessaly and Epirus.

December to February, and is generally in the form of light and continuous rain, rather than snow. Snowfall does occur at higher elevations in the interior, however. Temperatures during these mild winters rarely fall below freezing, and averages are in the upper 40s and lower 50s (degrees Fahrenheit, or 10°C). Summer temperatures are considerably warmer. Daily highs often average in the 80s (mid-to-upper 20s°C) and occasionally will reach into the upper 90s (mid-30s°C).

On very rare occasions, temperatures climb to and above a scorching 100°F (38°C). During recent years, Europe has experienced unusually severe heat waves. In some Mediterranean countries, including Greece, the weather took a serious toll, killing many people. One reason for the hardship and suffering is the European attitude about air-conditioning. For some unknown reason, Europeans have never accepted air-conditioning. This dislike, of course, is quite the opposite of Americans, who have enjoyed the comfort of artificially cooled air for decades. Perhaps it is because of the European myth that being exposed to air conditioners promotes sickness and generates poor health. This provides a wonderful example of the way in which culture, not the physical environment, influences our behavior and decisions. Today, the attitude is changing, partially in response to growing tourism. Visitors to Greece and other Mediterranean countries now often have the luxury of an air-conditioned room when they rent an apartment, or house, for their summer vacation.

With increasing elevation, climate gradually changes, becoming more continental. Winter temperatures are lower, precipitation is somewhat higher, and seasonal changes are more noticeable than along the coast. Because of its small size, no place in the country is more than about 50 miles (80 kilometers) from the sea. This means that the continental conditions mentioned earlier occur only in the northern mountainous regions. One characteristic of mountainous countries such as Greece is that they have considerable variations in climate, which results in variations in plant life. Temperatures, of course, drop with increased elevation and moisture often increases. One can experience these changes by driving even short distances from coastal tourist resorts into the countryside and higher elevation. In the mountains, it can often become unpleasantly chilly even during summer evenings.

ECOSYSTEMS

Ecosystems—a region's plant and animal life and water features—are influenced by climate more than any other natural factor. All life-forms have a natural habitat; an environment in which they can survive. Therefore, each plant and animal species is found in certain climatic conditions and absent in others. In terms of vegetation, the Mediterranean climate is characterized by a lack of continuous forests; rather, flora is dominated by shrubs, brush, and grasslands.

In Greece, as elsewhere throughout most of Europe, native vegetation was heavily disturbed by human activities. Clearing land for agriculture, cutting woodlands for timber, and extensive overgrazing by livestock all took their toll. In fact, because of these and other changes introduced by human activity, little if any of the original "natural" vegetation exists anywhere on the continent today. Today, the Greeks are beginning to preserve their remaining vegetation; they are more concerned with income gained from tourism, and few tourists want to see barren hillsides!

Greece's flora is well adapted to the existing climatic conditions, which includes high temperatures and long periods of severe drought during summer months. Because of these conditions, plant life in the Mediterranean climate is subject to scorching fires on a fairly regular basis. In order to survive, plants must become invulnerable to damages from direct exposure to reoccurring wildfires. This adaptation process among some plants is very interesting. For example, some species, such as various pines, must be exposed to fire in order to reproduce. They are known as pyrophitic (fire resistant) plant species. Other species successfully preserve water during summer months in order to avoid fatal exposure to drought. These plants, found in Greece as well, are known as xerophytes.

The countryside landscape also includes a variety of cultivated plants. Greece is known for its citrus fruits, wine producing vineyards, and olive trees that produce olives from which olive oil is extracted. At higher elevations, the landscape changes to uncultivated species of pines, beech, cypress, and other trees and shrubs. Many plant species found in this country are endemic, meaning they are found only in Greece.

For the most part, animal species inhabiting the countryside are related to other fauna commonly found in Europe, although some Asian species are present, as well. As is true in many other parts of the world, economic development and expansion of settlement drastically reduced the habitat of many large mammals. Bears, for example, exist but are limited in distribution to more mountainous and isolated northern areas. Few species pose a hazard to humans, although there are poisonous snakes. Vipers, the deadliest snake in the Mediterranean region, thrive here and can often be seen warming up or resting on limestone rocks on a sunny day. In order to prevent further reduction of endangered animal species, the government has created conservation programs and established national parks. Ten national parks currently occupy more than 100,000 acres (4,050 hectares) of land. The surrounding seas contain a bounty of marine life, including many edible species of fish and shellfish.

ENVIRONMENTAL PRESERVATION AND HAZARDS

Humans must be stewards of the natural environment. A close correlation exists between the quality of the environment and the quality of human life. Geographers have long recognized that most severely degraded environments also are home to people experiencing a very poor quality of life. A clean and protected environment, some scholars believe, is a luxury that only an affluent society can afford. Careful management of an environment and its resources requires a considerable amount of formal education (environmental awareness), environmental ethic (a desire to preserve, rather than exploit), time, and financial resources. Economic development sometimes acts as a double-edged sword: An expanding economy helps people live better initially, yet at the same time fast economic and population growth may damage the environment. Athens, one of the largest European cities, has been the destination of many Greeks searching for a better life. Because one in every three citizens of Greece currently lives in the quickly growing Athens area, the city battles choking air pollution. Haziness overrunning the city and famous classical architectural landscapes can be seen from miles away. This is a problem common to many large urban areas worldwide and is difficult to overcome.

Natural hazards are the various dangers nature presents to humans. At least that is how they are defined. Yet geographers recognize that in reality it is culture, rather than nature, that exposes people to natural hazards. It may be difficult to grasp this philosophical concept at first, but begin by imagining for a moment two different cultures living in a "treacherous" environment. Based on beliefs, customs, traditions, and so forth, each of them will develop different environmental perceptions. One may see floods as a permanent danger and decide to relocate in order to avoid their recurring damage. Another may simply accept flooding as something over which they have no influence. Their belief system explains such events as an act of god(s); something that will occur regardless of where they live. We choose where to live, often knowingly putting ourselves in potential danger (for example, living along active fault zones in California). Today, many hazardous events can be forecast and damage prevented by taking appropriate action. Often such warnings are simply ignored, though. Nature can be destructive, but it is humans, acting as cultural agents within their respective belief systems, that elect to place themselves in harm's way or remove themselves from potential hazards.

Greece faces the omnipresent threat of two potentially devastating hazards: volcanic eruptions and earthquakes. Currently, six of the country's volcanoes are active (can erupt at any time), and these are located on islands in the Aegean Sea. They pose a potential threat to everyone living within at least a 100-mile (160-kilometer) radius. Volcanic eruptions can eject huge amounts of scorching lava, ash, and gases. Earthquakes are earth movements that occur deep below the surface. They

Earthquakes are one of the most prevalent natural disasters that occur in Greece. Pictured here is the destruction left by the country's most devastating earthquake in recent years; one that hit Athens in September 1999 and registered 5.9 on the Richter scale.

can be devastating to land and structures built by humans, and they often take a heavy toll on life and property. Greece's most destructive earthquake struck near the outskirts of Athens in September 1999. About 150 people died, more than 35,000 homes were damaged or destroyed, and property losses soared to billions of dollars.

Wildfires present a clear and present danger for every Mediterranean country, including Greece. They happen during bone-dry summer months and can devastate natural vegetation, cultivated fields, and even settlements. Most of the fires are caused by humans, and many are set deliberately. Lightning occurs very rarely in the Mediterranean climate. One of the problems that affects the spread of fires is a limited amount of available water during the months of summer drought. Except for the Axios (Vardar) and Strimon (Struma) rivers, whose headwaters are deep in Macedonia and Bulgaria, few large streams flow through Greece's hilly countryside. It is not unusual to see dry riverbeds or small streams disappear into the rocky limestone-based ground and then reappear with autumn rains.

In summary, the natural environment sets the stage for human activities. Generally speaking, Greece has rugged terrain with little flat land, poor soils, little surface water, and a variety of potentially devastating hazards. In the following chapters, you will see how Greek culture overcame these obstacles to become a leading civilization of antiquity and how it earned a place among today's modern world nations.

CHAPTER

3

Greece Through Time

Human beings have occupied southeastern Europe since prehistoric times. Various human groups roamed the area for thousands of years, searching for good hunting grounds and places to gather food and establish settlements. Initially, these settlements were temporary stations for migratory groups. When people began raising plants and keeping animals, however, conditions changed drastically. The ability to produce and store foodstuffs in one place contributed to the creation of permanent settlements. This development, based on plant and animal domestication (the Agricultural Revolution), greatly improved people's quality of life. It also provided the foundation on which early civilizations were built. By 6,000 to 4,000 B.C., the mainland and islands of present-day Greece supported a significant population. Historically, this period correlates with the rise of early settlements in Mesopotamia and Egypt, and essentially the beginnings of what were to become the greatest of ancient Western civilizations.

At first, settlements were small and isolated and faced many geographic challenges. On the mainland, rugged terrain presented a serious obstacle to mobility. Mountain ridges made it difficult to establish transportation routes. Early residents of the Aegean coast naturally chose the sea as their primary means of connecting with people in other areas. They developed trade routes along seaboards and between islands. From early times, Greeks began turning to the sea, rather than the land, as their primary source of wealth and mobility. Geographers and other scientists interested in the diffusion (spread) of material culture have traced early trade routes in the eastern Mediterranean. They have been able to do so by analyzing the spatial distribution of pottery, jewelry, and other archaeological artifacts. Such research strongly suggests that to the Greeks and many other early peoples, the sea was a link rather than a barrier. The events just described took centuries to develop. Furthermore, people belonging to early cultures residing around the Aegean Sea were not of Hellenic (Greek) stock. Although they inhabited the region long before Greek tribes migrated southward, scholars are still working on trying to fit them into the right context.

FIRST CIVILIZATIONS

The earliest highly developed culture in what is now Greece was that of the Minoans, whose civilization flourished on the island of Crete during much of the second millennium B.C. Crete was well positioned to be the early crossroad of maritime trade routes in the eastern Mediterranean. It was the exchange place for goods from Egypt, the Aegean area, and Asia Minor. By 1,800 B.C., the Minoan civilization was the strongest naval power in the Mediterranean Sea. Abundant archaeological evidence suggests a high level of affluence in places like Knossos, a leading settlement. Lavish palaces, various types of

One of the first major civilizations that developed in Greece was that of the Minoans. Pictured here are ruins from a palace in Knossos, which is located on the island of Crete and once was the center of Minoan society.

pottery, jewelry with sophisticated ornaments, and a domestically created alphabet all provide evidence of a highly developed civilization. The Minoans even had the world's first indoor plumbing and roads that are still in use today!

History teaches us that no civilization, no matter how developed, survives forever. Even though the Minoan civilization was powerful, it was not powerful enough to recover completely from natural disasters such as earthquakes and the effects of nearby volcanic eruptions. Devastating earthquakes struck the island repeatedly, leaving entire cities in ruin. However, the ultimate decline of Minoan civilization came not from natural events but from cultural causes. The Minoans were victims of their own success. Because of their strategic location and tremendous wealth, they became a target for invasions by outside forces.

One invading group responsible for the Minoan decline was the Mycenaeans. This early Greek tribe built fortified cities and established a powerful civilization on the mainland about the same time the Minoan civilization was at its height. Eventually, their interests clashed and a conflict for dominance began. The Mycenaeans had a stronger and better organized military. By the mid-fifteenth century B.C., they had largely destroyed the Minoan civilization and its tangible landmarks. Cities lay in ruin, and the Minoan fleet was essentially destroyed, but many important Minoan culture traits, such as their art and alphabet, were adopted by those on the mainland. Mycenae (the Mycenaean fortified city) became the leader of the early Greek cultural realm and also held military control over much of the region's other cities and trade routes. Later on, when other Greek-speaking peoples moved southward, they found well-established urban settlements. These early civilizations, with their well-developed urban centers, provided the seeds from which Greek culture and civilization grew. Greeks would soon become the dominant force on the peninsula and throughout the Aegean region.

As is true of any civilization, the evolution of ancient Greek civilization was a lengthy process. In reality, it lasted more than 1,000 years, from the glory days of the Minoan civilization to the meteoric rise of the powerful city-states of Athens and Sparta. Migrations from the north happened in several stages. The best known movement of people was from 1,100 to 900 B.C., when the last wave of Greek tribes settled in their present-day homeland. It occurred as part of a larger migration, a chain reaction that eventually affected even remote areas of the Middle East and Egypt. This event was even recorded in the Bible as the "invasion of sea people" who permeated and settled coastal areas of Palestine. New arrivals meant changes in population and military capability. Despite technological supremacy and grandiose defensive walls around its cities, the Mycenaean civilization was eventually over-powered and gradually replaced.

For the next few centuries, Greece underwent a period of decline often referred to as the region's "Dark Age." Other than what is suggested by material artifacts, little is known about this period of Greek history. The situation is quite similar to the collapse of institutions in Western Europe beginning in the fifth and sixth centuries A.D. The recuperation period, recognized historically as the "Middle Ages," lasted several centuries. From what is known, Greece underwent a period of stagnation lasting from 900 to 700 B.C. In some respects, though, this should be viewed as a period of recovery rather than decline. For example, during this time, the Hellenic expansion began. The results of cultural interaction are tangible, particularly in preserved buildings and temples from that era built in Dorian architectural style (named after Dorian tribes, which led what became the Greek migration and occupation). Another even more important Dorian contribution was that they indirectly initiated the beginning of the gradual spread of Greek culture outside the Aegean region. Population growth in the homeland encouraged further migration into new lands.

GREEK CULTURAL EXPANSION

Around 700 B.C., Greeks began colonizing all sectors of the Mediterranean Sea and beyond. Population growth, combined with unsustainable agricultural practices, were driving forces behind the formation of hundreds of settlements, stretching from present-day Spain to what is today the country of Georgia. Greek city-states would send colonists to establish settlements overseas. Once they had gained a foothold in a new land, the Greeks initiated agriculture and trade with locals. They also engaged in many other aspects of cultural interaction and exchange. During the next two centuries, these colonies greatly expanded the Greek cultural region and

Hellenic way of life, reshaping the lives of many native populations. For the first time in European history, many different geographic areas enjoyed a form of cosmopolitan lifestyle under the umbrella of Hellenic culture.

Religion was one of the most successful tools used by the Greeks to peacefully spread their cultural influence. Geographer Dan Stanislawski noted that in order to establish better economic connections throughout the Mediterranean, Greeks would introduce a cult of the wine god Dionysus whenever they made contacts with local merchants. Gradually, worship of Dionysus became widespread among not just those involved in trade, but many others. Eventually, worship of the god of wine brought Greeks and non-Greeks closer together.

Of all colonies, those in Asia Minor (peninsular Turkey) were the most developed. Coastal areas of present-day Turkey were in close proximity to Greece, and the environments were very similar. One new settlement was built in 667 B.C. on the European side of the Bosporus Strait by colonists from the Greek mainland. They named it Byzantium, but it would eventually become known as Constantinople (present-day Istanbul, Turkey)—the world's greatest city for 1,000 years.

Toward the end of the sixth century B.C., the political fortunes of Asia Minor began to change. Increasingly powerful Persian kings were determined to conquer the known world. After gaining control of the Middle East, they turned their attention toward Asia Minor and Greece. For the next several decades, a Persian threat hung over the Greeks. Huge Persian military forces, often numbering several hundred thousand troops, defeated weaker Greek forces and pushed ever deeper into Greek territory. At this time, however, Greece was not one continuous empire. Rather, it was a large number of widely scattered, autonomous city-states (polis). The Greeks managed to regroup their forces for a final defensive stand against the Persians. In 490 B.C., at the Battle of Marathon (on the Greek peninsula), and later in the Battle of Salamina, the Greeks were

This map depicts Greece and the colonies it held circa 500 B.C. During this era, Greece held sway over parts of present-day Turkey and Italy, and repeatedly turned back threats from the mighty Persian Empire.

victorious. The tide began to turn, and soon the Persians were expelled from European soil for good. A century and a half later, when their forces collided again, the roles were reversed. The Greeks, led by Alexander the Great, marched toward the Persian capital and eventually conquered their empire.

Before Greece became a part of the Macedonian Empire of Philip II and his son Alexander III (also known as Alexander the Great), a century and a half of the most interesting period in ancient Greece's history would pass. It was the period during which art and science flourished. Cosmographers (early geographers) such as Herodotus recorded their observations about the *ecumene* (inhabited world). Artisans built palaces, temples, and exquisite statues of gods. Playwrights wrote wonderful dramas. Philosophers such as Plato and Aristotle produced classical works that are still considered masterpieces. Much of what we cherish today as the legacy of ancient Greece was created in the fifth and fourth centuries B.C. Athens, which eventually overpowered all political competitors, including its main rival Sparta, became a center of the Hellenic world.

THE AGE OF EMPIRES

Success and wealth attracts those who want it for themselves. In the case of the Greeks, it was a man whose appetite for conquering the rest of the world was greater than any in previous history. Many consider Alexander the Great of Macedonia to be *the* greatest conqueror in the history of the world. Macedonians led by Alexander's father, Philip II, conquered and unified Greece. Alexander (356–323 B.C.) continued on this path, and by the time of his death he was ruling over the vast lands between southeastern Europe, Egypt, and India. With every military expedition, Greek culture followed. Alexander was in many ways not just a conqueror but a unifying force, as well. His policies were to incorporate lands into his empire and have people benefit from Greek culture. Like no one before or after, Alexander had a habit of establishing cities named after him. Many of those cities still bear his name, the best known being the Egyptian city of Alexandria.

Greeks were known as "people of the book." They respected and appreciated learning, which is why they were welcomed almost everywhere as merchants and scholars. The Greek language was one of the earliest forms of international communication. It was an ancient *lingua franca*, a language spoken by peoples of different language backgrounds who need a common language for diplomatic and economic purposes. The Greek presence was felt in places as distant as the mountains of Afghanistan and India, where the memory of Greek culture and even some Greek cultural traits lingered for centuries. British military commanders reaching Afghan villages from

India in the nineteenth century were surprised to learn that in some of them, residents traced their lineage to the Greek residents of ancient Bactria (an old kingdom in Afghanistan).

Not long after the decline of Macedonian rule, Greece became a part of another empire, which would rule for many centuries. By the mid-first century B.C., well-organized military units of the Roman Empire were already controlling most of the Greek homeland. This marked the beginning of an interesting relationship; one in which political power and organization came from Rome, but most other aspects of culture were being accepted from Greeks. In fact, Romans eagerly and effectively integrated many elements of Greek culture into their own. This exchange is evident in "Roman" art, literature, and architecture, which were all heavily influenced by Greek culture. The Greeks, meanwhile, were content to be members of the cosmopolitan Roman Empire, the boundaries of which encompassed the Mediterranean world. For the next four and a half centuries, Greece was a part of the Roman Empire. Beyond the feeling of belonging to a vast empire, however, the Greeks did not really benefit from their role in the alliance. All roads led to Rome, not to Athens. Greece gradually became a remote province that was fast losing its charm and glory.

By the fourth century A.D., the Roman Empire experienced internal struggles and a general decline in its power. A few strong rulers such as Constantine managed temporarily to keep a tight grip. As an emperor, Constantine made two major contributions. He made Christianity the official religion of the Roman Empire. Also, in 330 A.D., he relocated the empire's capital, moving it to the city of Constantinople, thereby shifting the source of power and wealth into a Greek-speaking region. With these two decisions, Constantine single-handedly changed the course of Greece's people and culture for the next 16 centuries.

The relocation of the capital from Rome to Constantinople resulted in a great increase in the organization, power, and

In the fourth century A.D., Roman emperor Constantine established Constantinople (present-day Istanbul) as the Eastern Roman Empire's capital. Over the next millennium, the city was not only the center of the Greek-speaking world but also was the richest and most powerful city in Europe during the Middle Ages. Pictured here is Hagia Sophia, which was built in the sixth century A.D. and is the city's most famous structure.

influence of the eastern half of the empire. When the Roman Empire finally broke into eastern and western sections 65 years later, Greece became part of the stronger Eastern Roman Empire, which in various forms survived until the fifteenth century. For most of that time, it was a strong player on the geopolitical scene of southeastern Europe and Asia Minor, while preserving Greek culture there. The Western Roman Empire was weak. In fact, a century after the split, it was destroyed by advancing German tribes. Because of its ability to prevent permanent intrusion and settlement of Slavic and Germanic tribes into Greece, the Eastern Roman Empire (known incorrectly as the Byzantine Empire) preserved

Greek cultural dominance and their national identity on the Aegean Peninsula.

The rise of Constantinople also generated a power struggle between the pope of Rome and the patriarch (archbishop) of Constantinople. This struggle continued for centuries until Christianity finally broke into two separate groups, in 1054: Roman Catholic and Eastern Orthodox. All lands under the influence of the Eastern Roman Empire, which included Greece, became a part of Eastern Orthodox Christianity. If anyone knows anything about the history of southeastern Europe, he or she certainly knows how important religion is to people living there. In the political context, for example, Eastern Orthodox religion was often used as a tool for Russia to generate support from Greeks, Serbs, and others against its enemies. In recent years, Greeks publicly supported Eastern Orthodox Serbs during the Yugoslav ethnic wars.

MIDDLE AGES AND TURKISH OCCUPATION

During the turbulent Middle Ages, when much of Europe was in disarray for several centuries, Greece was the place where successful preservation of knowledge took place. During its zenith, Constantinople was the richest and one of the largest cities in the world. At a time when Rome and Paris were surrounded with swamps and peasantry, Greek cities managed to preserve ideas and teachings of great classical scholars. Centuries later, this knowledge eventually found its way to Italy and Western Europe, where it helped inspire the dawn of the Renaissance period. During much of the Middle Ages, prior to falling under Turkish control, Greece and the Eastern Roman Empire were the bellwether of European civilization.

By the eleventh century, another danger appeared. It came from the direction from which Persian armies had marched 15 centuries earlier. Turks, a group of nomadic tribes originally from Central Asia, had begun migrating westward, all the way to Asia Minor. First, Seljuk Turks and later Osman Turks gradually weakened the Eastern Roman Empire until 1453, when even Constantinople fell into Turkish hands and was renamed Istanbul. Turks continued marching westward, ultimately occupying all lands in southeastern Europe. All Greek lands, mainland and islands, became a part of the Turkish cultural sphere. Although Turks accepted many Greek cultural traits, the basic difference was religious. The Turks were Muslim and the Greeks were Christian. Muslims were hardly welcome in a Christian land, and being Christian in the Ottoman Empire (as the Turkish state was known) was not without its difficulties, either. As Christians, Greeks had to pay higher taxes and their children had to serve in the Turkish army. There were many other regulations that generated ill-feelings; after four centuries of Turkish occupation, these grew to be substantial.

Under Turkish rule, Greek development remained rather stagnant. As elsewhere in southeastern Europe, the economy was dwindling rather than developing. During this time, Western Europe was on the brink of the Industrial Revolution, an event that would once again move the center of civilization westward. Fortunately for Greeks in the eighteenth and the beginning of the nineteenth centuries, the Ottoman Empire was not the force it once was. Its power was rapidly declining, which made room for nations to push for independence. Following the example of other nations in their search for independence, Greeks started an uprising against Turkish rule in the 1820s. In 1832, after substantial bloodshed, they broke free of Turkish rule. At that time, not all present-day Greek lands were included in the newly independent state. Although decades later, the Greeks had to fight new wars to regain portions of their former territory, it was the beginning of a modern Greek state.

INDEPENDENT GREECE

The goal of uniting all Greek territories into one state was not an easy task. In this instance, geographical location was in many ways a curse. World powers had always wanted to gain a foothold in this extremely volatile and strategic corner of Europe. Great Britain and France did not want Russia to gain access to the Mediterranean region. Russia, meanwhile, was counting on its Greek friends to help them oust the Turks from Constantinople. Toward the end of the nineteenth century, Bulgaria and Serbia were both independent and eyeing their own territorial expansion southward toward Greece. Conflict once again loomed just over the horizon.

The early twentieth century brought exactly that—conflict. First Greece, Serbia, and Bulgaria went to war against the Turks and defeated them in 1912. A year later, Greeks and Serbs joined forces against the Bulgarians, resulting in the acquisition of additional territories. In 1914, World War I broke out with Greece and the Ottoman Empire on different sides. Vast numbers of ethnic Greeks still lived outside the Greek home-land, a majority of them residing in Asia Minor. For joining anti-German forces, Greece was promised western Anatolia, but instead it ended up in an unsuccessful war with Turkish revolutionary forces (under the command of Kemal Ataturk) that lasted from 1918 until 1922. As a result of this conflict, the Greeks lost an opportunity to incorporate their compatriots from Asia into one country. Most ethnic Greeks in Turkey (as well as Turks from Greece) experienced voluntary and "recommended" relocation that was little more than ethnic cleansing. After the war with Turkey, Greece's current geo-graphic boundaries were established.

CHAPTER

4

People and Culture

All geography is essentially cultural geography. Geographers, after all, study the spatial distributions and patterns of who is doing what, where, and why. They also are interested in knowing and interpreting the results of the human imprint on Earth's surface, the cultural landscape. Why people do certain things in certain ways (which are often unique to the particular group) is a primary interest of cultural geographers. The most important aspects shaping the lifestyle of each cultural group are its peoples' sense of belonging (ethnicity, religion, society, and so forth), language, education, diet, and demographic factors (also, political systems and economic activity, both of which are important enough to treat in separate chapters). Once you are familiar with major cultural characteristics of Greece's residents, you can decide for yourself what it is that makes Greeks similar to other people in some ways and much different in others. It is these aspects of their way of life that make them a distinct culture.

ETHNIC GROUPS

As emphasized in the previous chapter, for a variety of historical reasons Greece is a relatively homogenous country in ethnic terms (most of the people are from the same ethnic background). Considering that the Aegean Peninsula has served as a bridge linking Europe and Asia since ancient times, one might expect greater ethnic diversity. The tremendous ethnic diversity of its northern neighbors in the former Yugoslavia is well known. There, many groups share living space in close proximity. In Greece, ethnic diversity occurs on a region-to-region basis. The Greeks have a very strong sense of nationalism (of "being Greek"). Because of this feeling, ethnic issues are often a matter of heated political debate. Ninety-eight percent of the country's people are ethnic Greeks (that is, of Greek cultural heritage). In order to preserve ethnic homogeneity in their country, Greek public opinion often is very critical of other people who express a desire to be something other than ethnic Greek. They are afraid that if people are allowed to assume a non-Greek (that is, their own traditional) identity, it may cause problems. They may even seek to become politically independent, as was the case with the many ethnicities in the former Yugoslavia. Consequently, trying to suppress the recognition of ethnic Macedonians, in the eyes of some people, for example, means not having to deal with potential ethnic separatism.

This view, of course, certainly is not uniquely Greek. In fact, it is found elsewhere in Europe. Just across the border in Bulgaria, a similar "solution" was introduced to prevent the country's Turkish minority from officially becoming ethnic non-Bulgarians. These forms of extreme nationalism are cruel and discriminatory. Yet it is important to understand why they occur and how they affect a country's citizens. This is particularly true for Greece. A strong sense of nationalism

For a nation in which 98 percent of its citizens are ethnic Greek, the preservation of Greek culture is extremely important. For example, members of the Greek infantry who guard the Monument of the Unknown Soldier in Athens's Syntagma Square wear traditional Greek clothing.

(self-identity as a nation of peoples) should be expected in a country that has a history of turbulence, civil wars, dictatorial governments, and territorial disputes with neighbors.

THE PEOPLE

So who are the people living in Greece today? What is their background? How do the country's citizens differ from one another in terms of culture and self-identity?

Ethnic Greeks

Today, Greeks are really a mixture of many peoples who, throughout thousands of years, came to and left their mark on the Aegean Peninsula. Originally, however, Greeks were an Indo-European tribe, a stock having ancestry common to many peoples dispersed throughout much of Eurasia. People identified as Indo-Europeans are generally believed to have come from Asia Minor (peninsular Turkey) during the Neolithic period (perhaps 7,000 B.C.). From there, they migrated in many directions, eventually reaching the Russian steppes in the north and India in the east. Scholars were able to track these migrations by following the evolution and spread of the Indo-European language. Even though no one speaks original Indo-European, of course, the linguistic roots were preserved. This is how Greeks were identified as people of Indo-European stock. Interestingly, the Greeks are not ethnically related to any of their neighbors, most of whom migrated to southeastern Europe long after the Greeks were already established there.

Initially, the languages spoken by Greek tribes settling the Aegean Peninsula were used to identify common ancestry; the same method was used to identify non-Greek peoples living in the region. Because they did not migrate as one single group, but through the series of migrations over time, ancient Greeks had to figure out who they really were. Another cultural indicator that helped identify Greeks was their religion. Only Greeks worshiped the pantheon of gods led by Zeus, the supreme god in ancient Greek mythology.

Contemporary Greeks do not question their direct lineage from their ancestors. Most Greeks will argue, and rightfully so, that they are direct descendants of ancestors who fought Persian or Roman invaders 25 centuries ago. Greeks take great pride in their heritage and ethnicity, no matter where they live. Many Greeks have lived outside their homeland for generations, yet their sense of ethnic belonging remains as strong as that of Greeks living in Greece. This strong attachment to their traditional culture can be seen in many large North American cities. One only needs to visit a Greek restaurant that has been in the hands of a single family for several generations to witness the strong attachment to the homeland and its cultural traditions.

Because of various circumstances, ranging from wars to widespread poverty, Greeks have long experienced one of the highest emigration rates in Europe. In descending order based on percentages of national population, Greeks, Irish, Italians, and Croats have produced the greatest number of migrants. Most of those sharing Greek ancestry today live in traditional emigrants' havens of the New World such as the United States, Canada, and Australia. After the military conflict with Turkey ended in 1923, large numbers of displaced Greeks found new homes in the New World. Perhaps the best known of these refugees was Aristotle Onassis. After leaving Turkey, his family moved to Argentina, where he eventually became one of the world's richest men, with a fortune built primarily on shipping, oil, and the airline industry.

In the decades following World War II, thousands of ethnic Greeks left the country to search for better jobs in Western Europe, primarily Germany. War-ravaged Germany demanded more labor than its own population was able to support. For most immigrants, their jobs were supposed to last only temporarily. Today, however, many times two or even three generations of German-born Greeks reside in this country. This is often the case among migrant groups. Even though nostalgia and a strong desire to return home are important, the opportunity for economic success is an even stronger motivation. In the region around Greece, most ethnic Greeks living outside of their homeland reside in two countries, Albania and the island of Cyprus.

Ethnic Non-Greeks

In Greece's northwestern provinces, Albanians are the main ethnic minority. Some of them have been living in mountainous areas for centuries. Others arrived more recently as immigrants searching for better paying jobs than those available in their homeland. (Albania is the poorest European country.) Even though Albanians and Greeks are immediate neighbors, ethnically they are unrelated. Their only link is that at some time in the distant past, both groups had Indo-European ancestors. Albanians, however, are one of southeastern Europe's oldest inhabitants. It is believed that they descended from the Illyrians, who in a series of migration waves settled in what is now Albania around 1,200 B.C. Internally, Albanians are divided into two main groups. The Ghegs reside mainly in the north, whereas the Tosks are southern Albanians and make up the majority of Albanians who live in Greece. Greece's ethnic Albanian population, especially those who have been living in the country for generations, is mostly Orthodox Christian. It is estimated that perhaps a half-million Albanians currently live in Greece. Precise numbers are difficult to determine because of high and constantly rising rates of illegal immigration.

There are also ethnic Turks in Greece. The ancestors of modern-day Turks came from near the Altai Mountains, a region bordering Mongolia, Russia, China, and Kazakhstan. Turks were not just one ethnic group, either, but rather many groups of related tribes. Over a span of several centuries during the medieval period, several different tribes migrated westward and eventually established military control over local rulers. Their numbers were small at the beginning, but the Turks managed to incorporate many other peoples into their culture, thereby increasing their numerical strength through a process known as acculturation. People were willing to become "Turks" because of religion and other perceived cultural advantages. They do not share common ancestry with Indo-European peoples, but in Europe they are related to Hungarians and Finns. In Asia, they are related to most ethnicities in Central Asia.

During the time of the Ottoman Empire, Turks were spread throughout the eastern Mediterranean and southeastern Europe. Once the empire declined in power, however, many ethnic Turks migrated back to Turkey. Between the time of Greek independence in 1829 and the beginning of World War I in 1914, a large Turkish minority lived in northeastern Greece. Present numbers are drastically lower, however, because of both voluntary and pressured population migration since 1923. Although official numbers are vague, it is believed that some 100,000 Turks still live in the Thrace region of Greece. Ethnic Greeks and Turks share—or, more realistically, do not share!—the living space on the island of Cyprus. Although this small island is now a separate country, it long had been traditionally Greek in terms of ethnicity and history. After Turkish military intervention in the early 1970s, Cyprus was divided into two ethnic and political zones, one Greek and one Turk.

For official government purposes, Greece is the country of Greeks (claimed to represent 98 percent of the population). Ethnic minorities are generally ignored, or officially declared to be Greeks. This is the case with the many Macedonians who live in the northern part of the country. Some Macedonians are of Slavic origin and related to those living in the country's neighbor to the north, the Former Yugoslav Republic of Macedonia. Because Greece does not recognize their minority status, however, these citizens "officially" do not exist. In addition, major urban centers are home to increasingly growing numbers of immigrants (legal and illegal) from African and Asian countries. As a member of the European Union, Greece is the first stopover on the road toward Western Europe. The country is an attractive first destination for many of those looking for a better life.

RELIGION

Most people travel to Greece for three reasons. The first group searches for a pleasant and scenic place to spend their summer vacations. The second group comes because of their interest in ancient Greek culture and its many artifacts. Finally, Greece is also a destination for those interested in religious landscapes and history, particularly those relating to Greek Eastern Orthodox Christianity. The majority of Greeks consider themselves Eastern Orthodox Christians. Their church is independent of any larger ruling body, although it is loosely tied to other Orthodox faiths and the ecumenical patriarch of Constantinople. The patriarch is the nominal leader of all Orthodox Christians. This is the primary difference between Orthodox Christians and Roman Catholics, who recognize the pope of Rome as their spiritual leader.

The country's cultural landscape displays a rich religious heritage. Even the smallest village in the remote countryside has a place of worship with dome-like rooftops and Greek crosses. Famous monasteries perched on top of steep hills and rocks in the province of Thessaly are well known. Monks have occupied them for 1,000 years. Today, these humble yet spectacular monasteries are a main tourist attraction in that part of Greece. A millennium ago, however, their main role was to provide solitude-searching monks with a refuge from the world. Monasteries of Meteora are tremendous architectural achievements. In early days, the only way to gain access was to wait for ladders to be brought down. Another option

Religion is an important part of Greek culture; more than 95 percent of the nation's citizens are members of the Eastern Orthodox Church. Pictured here are worshippers making their way into a traditional Orthodox church, which typically includes a dome-like rooftop and Greek crosses.

was to attempt to scale the steep cliffs, resulting in almost certain death for all but the most experienced climbers.

In northern Greece, another famous Eastern Orthodox landscape exists. The complex of almost two dozen monasteries located on the Mount Athos Peninsula is a remarkable scene. These monasteries do not belong exclusively to the Greek Orthodox Church. Some belong to other Eastern Orthodox faiths such as Russian, Serbian, or Romanian. Mount Athos, located not far from Thessaloniki, is a major pilgrimage site. Here, one can often see dignitaries from other Orthodox countries. In 2005, Vladimir Putin became the first Russian president to visit this location and pay his respects to Mount Athos.

A small number of Greeks belong to the Greek Catholic Church. All religious ceremonies and traditions in this church are of Eastern Orthodox origin. Because of historical conflicts, however, this faith is officially affiliated with the Roman Catholic Church and looks to the pope of Rome for leadership.

Most Turks living in Greece are Muslims and follow the Islamic teachings of the Prophet Muhammad. In their case, practicing a different religion is a way of preserving their own ethnic identity. Some Albanians living in Greece are Orthodox Christians, whereas others are Muslims. The latter group was relatively small throughout history, but in recent decades it has begun to grow rapidly because of increased immigration from Muslim Albania. Many Albanians, especially those who arrived from tribal areas of central and northern parts of their homeland, are only nominally religious. Many of them follow ancient tribal codes of honor.

As is true elsewhere in Europe, Greece has become increasingly secular during recent decades. Most contemporary Greeks rarely visit a church outside important religious holidays. Younger generations appear to be less religious than their parents or grandparents. Urbanization, popular culture, and growing individualism are some of the reasons for the advance of agnosticism and atheism. More and more people seem to consider religion more as a form of cultural heritage and celebrate it that way.

The Greek cultural heritage is significantly symbolized by the many temples built by ancient Greeks. Today these remnants are mainly of interest to archaeologists and tourists. Yet these temples remind us of pre-Christian times, when Greeks practiced different religious beliefs. Their religion was polytheistic, meaning they believed in many gods instead of a single unifying god. Different gods had different roles that people would respect and celebrate. Apollo was a sun god, Ares the god of war, Aphrodite the goddess of love, and so forth.

POPULATION CHARACTERISTICS

Demographic (demography is the statistical study of the human population) trends in Greece are the reflection of general trends shared by most European countries. Although many countries in Africa, Asia, and Latin America experience population growth, a majority of European postindustrial societies face the prospect of population decline. In terms of demographic changes, countries pass through several stages. At the beginning, both birth- and death rates are high, which keeps populations from expanding rapidly. This is a characteristic of rural agricultural (preindustrial) societies. Then, when society enters the industrial phase, death rates become much lower, but birthrates remain high. This is the stage most of the developing world is experiencing today. Finally, societies in the postindustrial stage (developed countries) experience low death rates and very low birthrates. When the final stage is reached, population growth is slow and can even decline if more people die than are born.

Rapid urbanization, increased formal education of women, and change from an industrial to postindustrial (service- and information-based economy) are some of the factors influencing Greece's current demographic trends. Younger people tend to marry late, or not marry at all, and have fewer children than previous generations. Lifestyle changes from agricultural (where children were considered the form of family capital) to postindustrial (cash economy) are directly affecting Greece's demographic picture. As elsewhere in the Western world, pursuing education, careers, and economic opportunities, rather than having larger families, are becoming a priority for females.

Young Greeks understand that in today's world, having more children also means a greater economic burden. Another important factor is migration from the countryside. Birthrates in rural areas are traditionally much higher than those of urban centers. In urban centers such as Athens and Thessaloniki, population growth resulting from births has become stagnant. Cities grow because of migration into them. Almost half of Greece's population, for example, lives in the Athens metropolitan area, but nearly all of the growth has resulted from in-migration.

The Greek population, like that in most of Europe, is becoming older. Today, the continent's life expectancy at birth is 80 years. If these trends continue during the next couple of decades, Greece will join those European countries that are battling population decline. Current fertility rates (the number of children to which the average woman will give birth) are below 2.1, which is the minimum to prevent natural population decline. It is obvious, then, that in order to manage population issues, Greece must find a solution that will allow it to avoid serious economic and political problems. Having too few young people creates a lack of laborers to support economic growth. One possibility is to encourage immigration to the country and to allow large numbers of nonethnic Greeks to find homes and work there. This will not be an easy task, however, because of the Greeks' strong desire to retain their country's ethnic purity.

Life expectancy at the time of birth continues to increase, which is why nearly 20 percent of the current population is over 65 years of age. Currently, the average age of life

Like many European countries, Greece has an aging population, but perhaps more troubling is the nation's low birthrate, which stood at 9.7 per every 1,000 persons in 2005. If the birthrate continues to trend downward, Greece won't have enough laborers to support economic growth in a country that has had a difficult time developing its rural economy.

expectancy is 79 years; although with further improvements in medicine and in general quality of life, we can expect that number only to keep climbing upward. As elsewhere, females live a few years longer than males.

DIET

It has been said that people's diet represents one of their most important cultural indicators. What people eat and the way they eat can provide a tremendous amount of information about local lifestyles. People eat what they are. Many customs and manners are reflected in diet, especially in rural areas where changes occur slowly. Diet is a great example of cultural diffusion; that is, a spread of food preferences from one culture group to another. In parts of Europe, Christians will eat different types of food than Muslims, who avoid pork. In some areas, beer drinkers are in the majority, whereas in others wine is the drink of choice. A similar situation exists in the difference between coffee and tea consumption.

Those living in continental areas away from the sea consume much more red meat and hearty meals. The Mediterranean diet, on the other hand, consists primarily of grains, fresh vegetables, fish and other seafood, and generous amounts of olive oil. This diet is very healthy; few Greeks or other Mediterranean people have diet-related illnesses or suffer from obesity.

Greece is well known for its fabulous cuisine, and the West is familiar with many Greek dishes. Most Americans, for example, would recognize pita bread, cucumber sauce, rice rolled in grape leaves, kalamata olives, various eggplant-based dishes including moussaka, and many other Greek delicacies. In addition to fish and other seafood, lamb is considered a staple meat. Sheepherding is a millennia-long tradition on both the mainland and Aegean islands, so it is not difficult to understand why lamb is Greece's favorite red meat.

One fine illustration of cultural association is baklava. This famous dessert is popular throughout southeastern Europe and the eastern Mediterranean, as well as in the United States. Although basically a pastry of flaky structure covered with a honey-based syrup, baklava is prepared in many different ways based on regional differences and dietary preferences. It is a wonderful example of how food shapes regional identities!

Because of their Mediterranean diet, Greeks generally avoid heavy meals that can cause high blood pressure and heart disease, a leading cause of death in the West. Olive oil and wine are known for having substances that, while consumed in moderation, provide substantial health benefits. Greeks love their olive oil and wine, both of which are consumed during nearly every meal. They also believe that good food prolongs life. Scientists who have studied the long-living population of the island of Crete agree. Cretans boast one of Europe's longest life spans, which nutritional scientists attribute to a good diet. They believe that there and on other Aegean islands, human longevity and low rates of heart attacks are directly related to what people eat and drink.

A typical Greek dinner includes delicious appetizers, salads, and a few main courses accompanied by a glass of wine and something sweet to finish the meal. In the Mediterranean region, people tend to enjoy late dinners and not hurry while dining. So many of us in the West consume food just to satisfy hunger, rapidly chewing large bites of deep-fried fast food of questionable nutritional quality, but Greeks "dine." Dinner, most Greeks believe, is a cultural and social experience; it is a festival for one's mouth, rather than the fulfillment of biological needs.

CHAPTER

5

Government and Politics

D
emocracy, a term of Greek origin describing the specific political system of rule by citizens, was something contemporary Greece acquired relatively late. It is rather paradoxical that the cradle of democracy was often the site of undemocratic regimes. The modern political history of Greece is rather complex. After a lengthy time of political turmoil, followed by periods of relative calm, the country is today a republic with a progressive democracy. Longstanding geopolitical issues, particularly with Greece's neighbors, seem to have subsided. In the past, Greece lived under the omnipresent threat of external, or even internal, military conflict. Today, these concerns are fading away, and Greece can concentrate its political attention more on economic issues and other ways of improving the life of its citizens. This is not to say that hardships of previous times are forgotten. In this part of the world, memories fade slowly when it comes to politics.

POSTWAR POLITICAL HISTORY

Greece came out of World War II shaken, but generally in much better shape than many other countries that experienced tremendous devastation and loss of life. Unfortunately, the country was experiencing mounting internal problems between opposing political factions. Shortly after Greece had been liberated from German occupation and the monarchy had been toppled, civil war erupted. As was the case in neighboring Yugoslavia, it was a confrontation between Communists and Nationalists. Each side believed it could lead the country into a better future; although in terms of political orientation, they were vastly different. In Yugoslavia, the internal political conflict and World War II occurred simultaneously. In Greece, the civil conflict erupted in 1946, after the Nationalists won the majority of votes in the elections.

Both Greek factions received outside support. The Communists were supported by Yugoslavia and the Soviet Union, whereas the Nationalist government received help from the West. Communist forces lost the civil war mainly because they received less internal support from the Greeks themselves. In addition, the attention of Yugoslavia and the Soviet Union was diverted from Greece by their own serious political confrontation. In the aftermath of the 1946–1950 civil war, Greece was left as the only non-Communist country in southeastern Europe (if Turkey is considered to be Asian). Its neighbors—Albania, Yugoslavia, and Bulgaria—all spent the next half century under various Communist regimes. Not surprisingly, Nationalist supporters of the Greek monarchy established strong ties to the West, which continued to provide help. Soon after, in 1952, Greece joined the new North Atlantic Treaty Organization (NATO), formed only three years earlier.

The country nevertheless remained somewhat divided, especially among those who had been directly involved in the civil war. Such polarization affected Greeks' daily lives during the 1950s and 1960s, creating a difficult political situation. The problem with civil wars is that their effects are felt for a long time. Rarely does their outcome provide successful long-term solutions that satisfy all parties involved. In Greece's sequence of governments following World War II, political antagonisms prevailed, despite gradual improvements in the country's economic base. Greeks, just as their Italian neighbors, often tend to reform governments and executive bodies. Sometimes changes happen through elections and other times through military coups.

Greece remained a kingdom until 1967, when a group of military officers organized to resist electoral changes. They removed young King Constantine II from power, who proved to be the last king to rule over the Greek people. The military took control of the government and ruled as a dictatorship that lasted until 1974. This dictatorship, as any other, was unable to lead the country in a positive direction for economic growth. Rather, military leaders supported what they know the best: preparation for armed confrontation in order to keep the country and people "united." In this case, it did not work. Eventually, military rule came to an end, leaving behind a sour note in Greek history and also a long-lasting political problem relating to the future of neighboring Cyprus.

MODERN POLITICAL CHANGES

After generals, colonels, and other officers finally decided that it was time to retreat, Greeks were eager to restore democracy. Few people wanted a return to monarchy, so soon afterward, a republic was proclaimed. One might question how a country such as Greece could become involved in a military dictatorship. The answer lies in placing domestic events in a global context.

During the 1960s, the Cold War was making many people, including the Greeks, a bit anxious and paranoid. The military believed the country was being led in a direction that was "soft" on communism. Some saw political intervention as the only way to ensure the country did not drift further to the left. History has proven time and time again that military leaders who become unelected civil heads of state rarely if ever place the well-being of the country's people as their top priority, however. Officers rule with force, make poor political decisions, and often are removed by force. A leader of Greece's military junta and later (in 1973) the country's president, Georgios Papadopoulos serves as an ideal example of such a leader. He tried to transform the country into a republic and become a president, yet he eventually was overthrown and imprisoned for life.

As a new democratic republic in the 1970s, Greece rapidly began building a political structure that remains in place today. Distribution of power was divided among legislative, executive, and judicial branches of government. Left-wing parties that previously opposed each other emerged as serious contenders in a free electoral process. One of those was the Panhellenic Socialist Movement (PASOK), which dominated Greek politics during the 1980s and was led by Andreas Papandreou. Greece achieved one of its primary economic goals in 1981 when it joined the European Union (then called the European Economic Community). That same year, the socialist government, led by PASOK, was elected to power for the first time. These changes were milestones in Greece's politics and economy. For the last two decades, PASOK has remained the country's most influential and powerful political party. It won the most elections and formed most governments in this period, even after Papandreou's death in 1996.

Distribution of Power
The Parliament

As for distribution of power in the government, Greece is structured similarly to most democracies, including the United States. Legislative, executive, and judicial branches basically share equal powers. The Hellenic Parliament represents the

The Hellenic Parliament represents the legislative branch of the Greek government and meets in the parliament building in Athens. Constructed in the 1830s, the building today also houses the offices of the president of parliament, the office of the prime minister, and the secretariat of the cabinet, among others.

legislative branch; it creates new laws and expands existing laws. Members of parliament serve as representatives of their electoral districts and are affiliated with political parties, which nominate them as electoral candidates. The electoral procedure, however, is different than in the United States, because Greeks use a type of proportional system. The U.S. system is designed on the winner-takes-all principle. That is, in order to win all seats, a candidate needs only one more vote than his competitor. Whoever comes second receives no mandate whatsoever. The proportional system not only allows the winning party's candidates to enter parliament, but also those parties whose members received a smaller number of votes. This system allows many more voices to be heard, because parties with a smaller number of members can compete, as well.

Although the system may seem to be ideal, because it promotes greater participation of smaller parties, this is not necessarily the case. In the U.S. system, anyone can become a candidate for office regardless of the status of his or her political party. The European model does not allow such flexibility, because candidates are nominated by their party leaders and put on the long list of candidates. Criteria for being nominated may be something less than fair and objective; the result being candidates are often selected on the basis of popularity, rather than expertise. Proportional systems rarely generate election victories of more than 50 percent. In order to form a government, political parties most often form compromising coalitions, whether at the national or local level. In the 2004 elections, the Nea Dimokratia (New Democracy) party won, with 45 percent of the votes, just ahead of PASOK, which had 40 percent.

As a member of the European Union, Greece also provides delegates to its legislative body, the European Parliament. Based on its population, each member country is permitted to provide a certain number of delegates to this legislative body. Compared to German, British, or Italian delegations, Greece has a relatively small, though nonetheless still influential, voice in shaping European political policies.

Executive Branch

Although Greeks elect their president, the prime minister holds the real executive power. Greeks still remember times when power was held by a single individual. Therefore, they prefer a system of leadership in which the president holds mainly ceremonial powers. These include appointment of ministers already confirmed by the legislature and call for new elections if the parliament needs to be dissolved in case of political deadlock. Everyday operations are in the hands of the country's prime minister, who nominates ministers and oversees the work of various ministries.

In order to function properly and have a successful impact on the development of the country, Greece's government creates ministries with the purpose of coordinating their domains. The council of ministers presided over by the prime minister is called a cabinet. For example, the Ministry of Tourism is in charge of promoting tourism and regulating political and economic decisions in that regard. All ministries report back to the prime minister, who then reports to parliament. If parliament is unsatisfied with the government's performance, it can cast a vote of confidence on the prime minister's performance. If the vote is negative, the president may then call for new elections. For such a procedure to be approved, parliament must be overwhelmingly against the prime minister. This is difficult to accomplish, considering that prime ministers are usually the leaders of the party with the highest numbers of delegates. A vote against the prime minister is, for many members, a vote against their own party.

Judicial Branch

The distribution of power is incomplete without a strong and efficient judicial branch. If courts are successful in overseeing the inequalities and abstractions of law, then a legal system functions well. The judicial branch is a body that can exercise control over the other branches of government in order to limit their ability to overstep their political authority. In daily political life, it is common for any group to attempt to "shape" the understanding of the constitution for its own benefit. The Supreme Court serves as the main regulator of correct interpretation of Greek laws. On lower levels, the judicial branch is organized through the structure of regular and appeals courts, which provide expertise on various issues not necessarily related to the constitution.

FOREIGN AFFAIRS

As has been noted previously, Greece's geographical and historical circumstances have contributed to complications in foreign policy, some of which still linger today. Hopefully, all issues with Turkey will finally be resolved in peaceful ways. Although the two countries have not engaged in an open conflict for a long time, the potential for conflict is always present. Both sides recognize the peril of conflict, but in this corner of the world, foreign policy is sometimes conducted with the full flame of nationalistic feelings, rather than with compromising tones. Turkey feels uneasy that Greece's islands are only a few miles from the Turkish mainland, and Greece feels uneasy that Turkey's territory is located only a few miles from Greece's islands.

Then there is the extremely complex political issue of Cyprus; without a doubt the biggest political obstacle between Greece and Turkey and one that is a concern of the European Union. Since the mid-1970s, when this previously independent eastern Mediterranean island was split politically on Greek (south) and Turkish (north) sides, unity was desirable but never achieved. For all practical purposes, Greek and Turkish Cyprus function independently and ethnic animosities have played a large role in the island's recent history.

Traditionally, Cyprus has mainly been populated by an ethnic Greek majority, and Greek Nationalists have clung to the belief that the island is an integral part of Greece. Neither Cyprus's ethnic Turkish minority nor Turkey agrees. After three decades, the island is still divided into two political entities separated by a fortified buffer zone under United Nations' control. The Greeks have often asked for reunification, an idea the Turks have repeatedly rejected. However, in recent years, the Turks, under pressure from the European Union (it wants Cyprus unified), now support unification. Greeks recently rejected this option, however—they do not want to share the land with the poverty-stricken Turkish north. The future of Cyprus continues to be uncertain.

Cyprus is divided into Turkish and Greek sections: The Greek-controlled and internationally recognized Republic of Cyprus occupies the southern two-thirds of the island, while the Turkish Republic of Cyprus makes up the northern one-third of the island (a map of which is displayed on the building on the right). Pictured here is the boundary between the two states at Lidras Street in Nicosia.

The future relationship between Greece and the Former Yugoslav Republic of Macedonia is another ongoing problem. Greece has opposed its northern neighbor's claim to use the term *Macedonia*, because it has a northern province of the same name. More importantly, however, the name change could create separatism and future land claims by the Republic of Macedonia against Greek territory.

There are also burning issues between Greece and Albania. The rapidly rising numbers of illegal Albanian immigrants and the low status of the ethnic Greek minority in Albania are among the reasons for a strained relationship between the two countries. Greeks, believing that they have learned a lesson from the events in Serbia, are wary about the potential possibility for future Albanian political demands against their territory.

The relationship between Greece and the United Sates is productive and without major difficulties. Differences and disagreements do, of course, exist. Because of opposing public opinion, Greece did not support the United States–led war against Iraq. On the other hand, Greece is a member of NATO and highly cooperative with the United States and other Western powers, especially in the prevention of terrorist activities.

CHAPTER

6

Greece's Economy

conomy is an important element of culture. In order to survive and progress, each country must consider economy its highest priority. We all want to live better than did previous generations. Improving the quality of life of its people and transforming society from folk (traditional, largely rural) to popular (contemporary and largely urban) culture is, has been, and continues to be a major task for the Greek government. The pathway to economic development, however, is often full of obstacles that are difficult to overcome. How did Greece accomplish its current level of development? Which of the nation's goals were achieved and which were not? Questions such as these are answered in the following overview of Greece's economic geography.

DEVELOPING ECONOMY

Despite numerous political issues (see Chapter 5), Greece

benefited substantially from the Cold War confrontation between the East and West. Western Europe did not want a regime change that would shift the balance of power in the eastern Mediterranean. It was firm in its stand against the Soviet Union gaining an exit to the Mediterranean. Supporting Greece economically meant better political ties as well. Pragmatists in the European Union (at that time known as the European Economic Community, or EEC) decided that Christian Greece would be a more acceptable member than Muslim Turkey. Even today, many of Western Europe's officials value potential membership on the basis of the "Europeaness" of potential candidates for membership.

After a politically turbulent period during the first part of the 1970s, Greece finally achieved internal peace during the second half of the decade. Soon after, in 1981, it became a full member of the EEC. For the first time in its history, the EEC accepted a country that did not directly border any of its existing members. At the time, Greece was separated from its nearest member, Italy, by the Ionian Sea, and for all practical purposes it was on the European periphery. In terms of geopolitical strategy, however, it was in the right location. Before joining this organization, Greece's economy was stagnating. A series of attempts at economic reform had been largely unproductive. It took decades to transform a traditionally agricultural society into a modern industrial society.

In the aftermath of World War II, Greece and other countries in the region faced an awesome challenge. To avoid falling into even greater lack of development and resulting poverty, Greeks had to modernize. Initially, the economic growth rate was significantly higher than that throughout most of Europe (boosted primarily by outside investors), but this was somewhat misleading. During the 1950s and 1960s, it was more a reflection of the fact that the starting point itself was much lower than that of Western Europe. In order to provide an economic stimulus, the government relied on borrowing from international sources. This, combined with political unrest in the late

1960s and early 1970s, caused Greece to move dangerously far from the right economic path. Fortunately, this downward spiral was reversed in 1981, when Greece became integrated with most developed European economies.

What Greece needed was an open door (and open boundaries) to a large market, but adequate direct land connections with the remainder of Europe were still unavailable. Having an opportunity to participate in this economic (and now increasingly political) integration was quite a boost for the country, yet membership was also somewhat of a double-edged sword. On one hand, Greece's economic productivity increased, and the service sector expanded considerably. Substantial financial support was received from the European Union for economic improvements. On the other hand, because Greece had borrowed heavily to fuel its economic growth, its internal and external debt increased substantially over several decades.

ECONOMIC SECTORS

Following World War II, agriculture gradually declined in economic importance. Today, although it is still important, it accounts for less than 10 percent of the gross domestic product (GDP). Primarily because of its rugged terrain, Greece is not ideally suited to large-scale agricultural production, unless it is a typical Mediterranean type of farming. Most of Greece's agricultural land is owned by small landholders who inherited their ancestral properties. The main products are fruits, olive oil, wine, and vegetables, which can be cultivated on small plots of land. In addition, because of the generally small scale of its farming operations, Greece is not in a position to compete successfully with Spain, Italy, and other Mediterranean agricultural competitors.

Agriculture has suffered for another reason. Young people are increasingly unwilling to work in traditional rural (including agricultural) roles. Rather, they move to cities that offer more amenities and excitement, as well as jobs in service-related

Olives are a staple among Greece's agricultural products and over the last decade are the only crop whose production has increased. In recent years, Greece has supplied between 5 and 8 percent of the world's olives; two-thirds of which is sent to European Union countries.

industries. As a result, the amount of land under cultivation has constantly decreased since the mid-1900s. Among agricultural products, only olives have increased in production during the past decade. On the positive side, ongoing developments in the food-processing industry may help revitalize at least some types of agriculture.

Today, most countries strive to develop a strong postindustrial or service sector, an indicator of technological progress and economic strength. Post-Industrialism involves a major economic transition: traditional economic activities such as farming, fishing, forestry, and mining aren't as important as they once were; neither are the secondary industries, such as manufacturing. Rather, most people are engaged in providing services. The service sector mostly requires people who are well educated, highly skilled, and able to work in a number of highly specialized fields such as teaching, management, medicine, law, and many other "white collar" trades. Today, about two-thirds of the Greek workforce is employed in the service sector, almost twice the number still working in primary or secondary industries.

Greece is currently moving toward achieving its goal of becoming a well-developed, postindustrial country. Obstacles remain, of course. One major problem is the unequal development of rural and urban areas. Much of the countryside remains poorly developed and impoverished. But even here, there is hope. Rural Greece holds great potential for further development of the country's tourist industry. Beautiful scenery, rustic landscapes, rural folkways and a slow pace of life draw many visitors away from the hustle and bustle of the country's urban centers. Millions of tourists are already attracted to the country's coastal and island scenery and its rich cultural heritage. In recent decades, tourism has become one of the leading sources of income from foreign capital, which totals about $10 billion annually, or about one-fourth of the service sector economy. Greece is also trying to capitalize on sport tourism, in which it has had a long and successful experience. For decades, major sporting events, including the 2004 Summer Olympics, have been conducted in Greece, usually in Athens.

As has been noted, both the primary and secondary sectors of the Greek economy are weakening. The country has very few natural resources, and mining and energy production from domestic resources are unable to meet even Greece's own needs. However, one area of the secondary economy is experiencing growth. The country's need to expand and otherwise improve on its infrastructure has generated considerable investment in the construction industry. Urban centers are in desperate need for the creation of better transportation net-works. Rural areas also require better transportation routes if they are to capitalize on their tourism potential.

TRADE AND LABOR

Membership in the European Union helped increase Greek exports to Western Europe, which is the main consumer of Greece's products. During the 1990s, civil conflicts in the territory of the former Yugoslavia severely disrupted the surface transportation of goods from Greece to Western Europe. Fortunately, the country's shipping fleet ranks among the world's largest, and transportation by sea was not inter-rupted. Outside of Europe, Greece's major economic partner is the United States, which accounts for roughly 15 percent of both its exports and imports.

Every country strives for a positive trade balance by exporting more than it imports. When the balance of trade is positive, the excess capital can be used to support government projects such as increasing public services, (re)building the nation's infrastructure, or simply saving it for the future. One of the problems developed countries often face, however, is that they sometimes spend more than they can afford. They import more than they export and have to find ways to provide enough cash to pay for that difference. This is called negative trade balance.

Because countries can survive on credit, they often borrow money from outside sources. Such a policy creates govern-ment and public debt that contributes to additional problems. Unfortunately, Greece suffers from a negative trade balance. The difference in 2004 was significant, with $15.5 billion of exports compared to a whopping $54.28 billion of imports. The Gross Domestic Product (GDP) was $198 billion in 2004 and experiencing steady growth. In the same year, however, the overall debt rose to over 10 percent higher than the actual GDP. The existing financial deficit is having a direct negative effect on Greece. As a member of the European Union, the euro is Greece's official currency and the country also must abide by EU rules. The body strictly controls (and punishes) governments that overspend and show a lack of fiscal discipline, and Greece is no exception.

Greece has been affected by the economic slowdown that most of Europe has experienced in recent years. Over the years, the country had reduced its unemployment rate, but by 2005, it once again climbed to a level of about 10 percent of the workforce. By EU standards, this is one of the Union's highest rates of unemployment, but compared to all of Europe (including former Soviet bloc East European countries), the number is average. Of particular concern is the gender gap in unemployment: For women, the figure stands at about 16 percent, whereas it is only 5 percent for men. This disparity clearly points to the need for economic reforms that will increase female representation in Greece's labor force.

Essentially, the wide gap in gender employment illustrates the difficulties created by Greece's traditional male-dominated sociocultural system. Women remained at home and were involved only in traditional domestic activities. On the other hand, men worked outside the home to provide resources to support their family. Only during the twentieth century did this system begin to change, yet such changes can be painfully slow in happening. Today, women are still paid less than men and have a harder time finding better paid positions (a situation common to many European countries). Why is gender so important when analyzing a country's economic indicators and labor force? The answer is simple: More than half of Greece's population and potential labor force are women. Theodore Schultz, a Nobel Prize–winning American economist, reminded us how investing in human capital is the single most important investment any country can make. If Greece is to prosper, it must rid itself of male social dominance and fully integrate its women into the workforce.

Although Greece's unemployment rate stood at 10 percent in 2004, the rate for women was much higher (16 percent). Another ongoing problem is that Greek women are paid substantially less and are often not integrated into a workforce still largely dominated by males. Pictured here are female Greek workers in Athens protesting the rate of unequal pay.

Another serious obstacle to economic development is the lack of full privatization of industry. Many large companies remain state owned, and they operate under strict control. When governments control businesses and industries, progress and expansion are often blocked by bureaucratic barriers. In the United States, nearly all business is owned by the private sector. By contrast, European countries, including Greece, tend to have a tighter control over some industries. The reason Europeans practice such a policy is because of the region's dedication to a welfare state. Governments, rather than private enterprises, provide many public services.

About two-thirds of the country's 4.3-million-person work-force hold jobs in the service sector. It is hardly surprising that more than a million of them are employed in professions related to tourism, hotel management, trade, and leisure activities. With the expansion of tourism in the foreseeable future, these numbers will certainly rise.

ENERGY, TECHNOLOGY, AND TRANSPORTATION

Per-capita energy consumption is the main indicator of a country's economic strength. The United States, for example, has only 5 percent of the world's population but consumes a quarter of the world's overall energy, far more than any other country. The U.S. economy is also the world's largest, by a considerable margin.

Greece's energy consumption has grown hand-in-hand with its economic development. The country, however, faces some serious energy-related obstacles. The recent skyrocketing fossil-fuel prices are generating serious consequences world-wide. Greece has few energy resources and must import over 90 percent of its petroleum from international suppliers. Currently, most of it is obtained from the Middle East, but the future prospect of receiving oil and gas from the former Soviet Union appears bright. Russia, a natural gas-producing giant, has been working on a European natural gas distribution network in order to become a leading supplier throughout the continent. Traditionally friendly with Russia, Greece seeks to ease its dependence on Arab oil, diversify its sources, and become less vulnerable to unexpected disruptions in supply.

Russian natural gas is already flowing to Turkey through a pipeline located deep in the Black Sea. Oil from the Caspian Sea is being transported through another pipeline to Turkey's port, Ceyhan. In both cases, Greece seeks an extension of these routes to its soil, whether by pipeline or tanker. Additional pipelines also are being built to connect Greece with its northern neighbors, Bulgaria and Macedonia. One of the projects in the works is a pipeline connection with Italy, across the Ionian Sea.

Most electricity is produced by plants powered by coal or natural gas. Greece has little if any hydroelectric potential and the government is not interested in venturing into nuclear energy. Many European countries, including Greece, are searching for ways to implement large-scale alternative means of generating electricity. In Greece, however, projects to develop solar and wind power are still in their infancy.

In the areas of transportation and technology, Greece lags far behind most of Western Europe and much of the rest of the world: Railroads and most highways are in need of upgrades and expansion, large urban centers suffer from massive traffic congestion, and in many communities, public transportation is inadequate. Here, once again, the primary obstacle is the slow transformation of governmental bureaucracy and state-controlled business operations. In telecommunications, the country's networks are in serious need of upgrading and expansion. If this trend continues, the information network could become well developed. Instead of trying to upgrade outdated networks, the emphasis is now on laying new fiber-optic cables and building a mobile telephone infrastructure. However, this is not an easy or inexpensive task in a country with so many islands and isolated places.

7

Regions of Greece

A s a country of relatively small size and inhabited by people who, for the most part, share the same ethnic and religious background, Greece is certainly less diverse than many other European countries. Regional differences here perhaps are not as sharp, yet they are noticeably significant. To many readers, it may seem odd that a country the size of an average U.S. state can actually have any noteworthy regional differences. In Europe, however, the array of cultural characteristics can change greatly from one side of a mountain to another. The explanation lies in a long history and the accumulation of cultural traits over a span of thousands of years. In Chapter 4, for example, it was noted that diet and cuisine can reflect regional differences and changes. Perhaps the greatest regional differences stem from the varying rate of socioeconomic change occurring in the country. Change comes slowly in rural areas that are dominated by people still practicing folk culture. Urban areas, on the other hand, experience a more modern way of life. These cultural differences are social, economic, political, and demographic.

EASTERN MACEDONIA AND THRACE

Eastern Macedonia and Thrace is located in the extreme northeastern part of the country. It represents one of the latest additions to Greece's territory. Located closer to Istanbul, Turkey, than to Athens, this province has traditionally been culturally linked more so to the former than the latter. At least that was the case until Greece and Turkey swapped some territory and exchanged ethnic populations in the years immediately following World War I. At one point in ancient history, Thrace was a kingdom that spread across much of southeastern Europe (including present-day Bulgaria and the European part of Turkey). Many ancient Greek sources mentioned Thracians and their kingdom. They, however, eventually became acculturated (assimilated) into Greek culture.

Today, Thrace occupies the picturesque eastern periphery of the province. (It is important to add that *Eastern Macedonia* is the province's western part and adjacent to Central Macedonia.) It lies between Bulgaria and the shores of the Aegean Sea and is the country's "flattest" province, although even here some mountain landscapes rise above the plains. In the past, agriculture and fishing were the main economic activities. Today, however, it is a region of emigration (out-migration), as many people migrate to cities in search of better jobs and higher wages.

Thrace is also one of the most ethnically diverse regions of Greece. Even here, Greeks are predominant, but Turks and Pomaks (a Slavic population who are Muslims but speak a Bulgarian language) are also present in large numbers. In terms of cultural geography, this is important, because the cultural landscape of rural Thrace reminds one of the long history of the local people. Visitors can notice differences in customs, manners, relationships, and so forth, just by taking a walk in ethnically mixed villages. Even though Thrace had previously experienced its fair share of culturally based atrocities, today ethnic harmony predominates.

CENTRAL AND WEST MACEDONIA

Only in this chapter on regions does the reader become aware of the importance of the name Macedonia in this part of the world. Macedonia(s) exists on several different political boundaries. Greeks, FYR (Former Yugoslavian Republic) Macedonians, and Bulgarians all believe that *their* Macedonia is the right one. The reality is that they are all the right ones and could not exist without each other. Greece divided its Macedonia into three provinces; Central Macedonia is the largest and best developed. Previously the core of Alexander the Great's kingdom and an important center of the Eastern Roman Empire, today this region is Greece's northern counterpart to Athens. Its physical landscape is a combination of hills and the river valleys of two of the largest streams flowing to the Aegean Sea, the Axios and Strimon.

Geographic location played a vital role in the cultural evolution of Central Macedonia. Both Greeks and Slavs left an impressive cultural imprint on the region. Nowhere is this imprint more obvious than in Thessaloniki, the cosmopolitan capital of northern Greece and, with a half-million residents, the country's second-largest city. Located on the shores of the Aegean, not far from the mouth of the Axios River, the city's location played a large role in helping it develop as a political and economic center in ancient times. Because of this role, however, the city was always a target for invaders. Romans, Slavs, Turks, and others plundered the city and left their own cultural imprint. Their presence can still be seen in the city's architecture and in displays in its many museums.

Today, Thessaloniki is an important seaport and transportation center of goods for northern Greece and neighboring

An important industrial and commercial center, Thessaloniki is the second-largest city in Greece. The city's harbor opened in 1901 and it serves as a distribution point for Greek agricultural products and raw materials.

areas of the former Yugoslavia and even central European countries. Economic prospects and other opportunities drove many rural Central Macedonians to Thessaloniki, where the majority of them reside. The countryside is less developed, with only a few larger urban areas, all of them remote from Thessaloniki. A good part of Central Macedonia is under agricultural cultivation, especially in lowlands created by the two rivers. There, one can see fields covered with fruit trees or tobacco plants, much of which is exported.

The West Macedonia province, a predominantly hilly and rural countryside of northwestern Greece, is the western extension of Central Macedonia. It is one of the less developed areas, with smaller municipalities, most notably Kozani, and a stagnating economic base. Some of the major obstacles in its development were its distance from leading Greek urban centers and proximity to even less productive regions of Albania and FYR of Macedonia. It has only about 300,000 residents, one of the lowest populations of any Greek region.

THESSALY

Farther south from West Macedonia is where the "real" Greece begins. Thessaly has been a well-known and important region since ancient times. It lies close enough to Athens to have benefited from its cultural and political reach. Its mountains were the home of gods: Mount Olympus, the highest mountain in Greece, was a vital place in ancient Greek mythology, because it was the place where the supreme god, Zeus, and his fellow gods resided. Mountains, however, aren't the only geographic feature of Thessaly. Actually, this area of Greece is known for its plains, which attracted settlers from the dawn of mainland Greek civilizations. Mountains can best be thought of as defining the province's borders, whereas plains form the central core.

These plains are well suited for agriculture, which is an important contributor to the local economy. Because of its geographic location in central Greece, the flatlands of Thessaly receive above-average precipitation in the summer, an essential factor for cultivating fruit and grain. The region is better developed than its northwestern neighbors, West Macedonia and Epirus. Another benefit of its geographic location is that it serves as a transportation crossroad between Greece's southern and northern regions. Main highways and railroads from Athens to Thessaloniki pass through Thessaly. This is especially beneficial for Larissa, the region's capital, economic hub, and largest city and its 140,000 residents, or about half of the province's population. The western boundary follows the Pindus Mountains, which form a natural boundary between Thessaly and Epirus. There, in the peaceful country-side, is one of Greece's main tourist destinations, Meteora, with its famous monasteries.

EPIRUS

In terms of accessibility, the province of Epirus lies farther from Athens than any other region of Greece. It is separated from the capital by the Pindus Mountains and historically has been relatively isolated from Athens. Culturally, of course, it was always Greek. In fact, it was home to Greece's second-most important oracle, after Delphi. The region's picturesque landscape holds many remains, testifying to its historical importance. Much of the province is mountainous and it is also the country's most forested area. The combination of rugged terrain, ample moisture, and forests has produced beautiful natural landscapes that many Greeks and foreigners come to admire. Because of its higher elevations, Epirus has also become a winter tourist destination, where visitors can enjoy downhill skiing.

In terms of cultural landscapes, the province is predomi-nantly rural, with a few small urban centers. Recent economic emphasis has been on the development of tourist facilities, although it will take time to catch up with the rest of Greece. The lifestyle in Epirus is very provincial, easygoing, and laid-back—in a very refreshing and positive way.

A serious obstacle to economic growth in Epirus is that neighboring Albania remains economically underdeveloped. This not only limits economic cooperation but also increases the number of immigrants crossing the border in search of jobs. A substantial Albanian ethnic minority has lived in Epirus for centuries, adding to the cultural diversity of northwestern Greece. With the sharp increase in Albanian immigrants, however, the region's economy is being stretched. Many residents are also becoming concerned about what they perceive to be unwelcome social changes. The leading city is

Ioannina, a regional economic and educational center with a long and rich cultural heritage.

CENTRAL AND WESTERN GREECE

Moving southward from Epirus, one notices the landscape change to strictly Mediterranean limestone-dominated mountainous terrain of two provinces—Central and Western Greece. Here, mountains rise abruptly from the sea, resulting in sharp changes in climate and ecosystems within very short distances. Central Greece is a transitional zone that reaches from the Ionian Sea to the Aegean coast, thereby dividing the country into two parts. To the north lies slower paced northern Greece, and to the south is the Greek cultural hearth of Athens and surrounding areas.

Central Greece even functions as a transitional place in some respects. For example, like the North American Great Plains, people usually pass through en route to somewhere else. One reason to stop is the region's archaeological treasures. The province is best known for having one of the most significant archaeological sites in Greece, the ruins of the famous Oracle of Delphi. In ancient Greece, people would go to the Oracle of Delphi to hear advice about their future. The site was highly respected and protected by gods and human rulers, thus being a place of peace. Many emperors would come to ask the Oracle about their destiny. Sometimes answers were positive and sometimes they were not, because it depended on interpretation.

The most famous story about a misinterpreted message happened when Lydian emperor Croesus asked for advice about the war against the Persians. Lydia at that time was a powerful empire in present-day Turkey. The message he received said that in the event of an attack on Persia, one great empire could end up being destroyed. Encouraged with the advice, Croesus attacked the Persians, and ultimately a great empire was, indeed, destroyed—his own. After the introduction

Located in the province of Central Greece on Mount Parnassus, the ruins of Delphi were designated a World Heritage Site by the United Nations Educational, Scientific, and Cultural Organization (UNESCO) in 1987. According to legend, Delphi was the home to the Oracle of Apollo, which ancient Greeks consulted to learn of their future.

of Christianity to Greece, the Oracle was terminated, because the tradition was considered an element of pagan culture. If, by some miracle, the Oracle of Delphi had remained in business until the present day, without any doubt its largest customers would be American stock-market speculators lining up to hear good news. At the same time, they would greatly increase Greece's income from tourism!

Generally speaking, this part of Greece is one of rural landscapes, with small and widely scattered small urban areas that serve as local economic centers. Here, as in other provinces, it was difficult to escape Athens's economic and political dominance and independently develop a strong economy. Unless they are located on main traffic routes, regional centers grow slowly. The leading city is Lamia, the region's economic center, with a population of about 75,000.

Western Greece differs little from Central Greece, both in terms of physical geography and cultural landscape. If one is interested in exploring the remnants of folk culture, this is the place to go. The countryside is a tapestry that reveals much about the historical past and cultural present of the local population. Tiny roads leading to picturesque villages wind lazily around the hills that separate quaint settlements that in some cases are thousands of years old. These charming landscapes so rich in history are particularly abundant on the Peloponnesus side of Western Greece.

PELOPONNESUS

At one point in history, when the Greek city-state of Sparta was a tremendous military power, the island of Peloponnesus was the place to be. That was 2,500 years ago. Since then, most of Peloponnesus has fallen into provincial obscurity. Rapid industrialization and urbanization in the post-World War II period bypassed most of the province, and many people left the region. Although it is not far from Athens, Peloponnesus appears to have benefited from this progress less than it should have, at least in theory. It often seems as though the four-mile-long Corinth Canal, which separates Peloponnesus (therefore making it an island) from the rest of Greece, is more than just a physical barrier. Clearly, being close to Athens, but not close enough, can mean stagnation rather than growth in Greece. Only one city, Patra, has 100,000 residents.

Nevertheless, Peloponnesus has plenty to offer, especially tourism, but competition with other provinces is keen. Despite having many ancient city-states, fortresses, and archaeological sites, tourist facilities are poorly developed on the island. With careful planning and investment, this region might become a significant tourist destination, hence, a greater contributor to Greece's economy. The coastal zone is a marine paradise, and rural tourism in remote villages, where people can wander through orchards, olive trees, and vineyards, can be equally profitable.

One obstacle to development is the tradition of conservatism. Many people on Peloponnesus cling to the past and are reluctant to change their way of life. This situation is common in areas where the transition from folk to popular culture has been slow. Rural people often fear changes to the existing cultural system, because change threatens the "traditional" lifestyle. In Greece, this conservatism hinders economic development. This is not exclusively a Greek cultural trait, however. It is common to most traditionally rural places. To picture this conservatism in the United States, we can think of the characteristics of "small town America."

ATTICA

During antiquity, it was said that "all roads lead to Rome," even those in Greece. In present-day Greece, the same can be said about Athens. To Greeks, Athens is a city of overwhelming importance, both historically and today. Its sprawling metropolitan area is home to half of all Greeks. The city is also Greece's economic, political, and social hub, as well as its center of popular culture. Athens and the port city of Piraeus make up most of Attica Province.

Athens has a very long and celebrated history. Established almost 3,000 years ago, the city has enjoyed an influential political and economic prominence throughout most of its existence. That existence was endangered many times by various invaders, yet Athens survived. During the Peloponnesus Wars against Sparta in the fourth century B.C., it was almost destroyed, but Sparta eventually lost and disappeared from the main stage of history. This is one reason why Peloponnesus declined in importance, whereas Attica rose to become Greece's leading region.

In recent times, especially after World War II, Athens boomed in terms of population and economic growth. Shipping links with the outside world are through the port of Piraeus, the artery through which goods are supplied to Athens or exported from the city to worldwide destinations. When most people think of Athens, though, the city's glorious past is what is most apt to come to mind.

This entire book could easily be devoted to Athens's cultural heritage and other aspects of its rich historical past. Whereas history is extremely important, in order to understand contemporary Greece, it is more important to think geographically, that is, spatially. Athens is a node (core) of a functional region. Its role in Greece is even more important than what Los Angeles means to Southern California or Dallas means to Texas. Economy, education, politics, and all other aspects of culture affecting Athens today will influence the rest of Greece tomorrow.

Having such a prominent capital city can be counter-productive to the rest of the nation, simply because the city receives the majority of attention. Political benefits, economic benefits, educational opportunities, and social amenities focus on Athens. In a country with limited resources, little is left to share with outlying provinces. Athens certainly ranks among the world's great capital cities. This was confirmed during the 2004 Summer Olympic Games hosted by the Greek capital in magnificent fashion. In preparation for the event, during the preceding decade the city underwent drastic improvement and modernization through large construction projects. These, of course, further diverted resources from the countryside.

THE GREEK ISLANDS

In some respects, the Greek islands define the country, at least in the mind of many non-Greeks. Hundreds of islands, each of them somewhat unique, surround the mainland. To an international traveler, island hopping is perhaps the most interesting way to experience Greek culture. Even today, on many islands one can step back in time by leaving tourist villages and visiting small communities that have experienced little change for centuries except, perhaps, for paved roads and electricity. Customs and manners are still part of the slowly changing cultural system designed in ancient times. A day or two later, a ferry takes you to another island and another village, which almost certainly will have its own characteristics and charm.

Greece's islands have been popular destinations for many generations of Western artists and writers in search of inspiration. They were drawn to the islands by their idyllic landscapes and the genuine simplicity of the Mediterranean lifestyle. These spectacular yet quaint landscapes are peaceful and breathtaking, but they also reflect centuries of economic hardship and cultural isolation endured by previous generations to whom the isolated islands were home. In his famous novel *Zorba the Greek*, Nikos Kazantakis, one of the greatest Greek writers, describes the cumulative expression of life on the island of Crete and its good and bad aspects.

Politically, the Greek islands do not belong to a single administrative province. Rather, some of them belong to mainland provinces, but most others, such as Crete, the North and South Aegean Islands, and the Ionian Islands, are self-administered.

The first major island group reached on the ferry trip from Piraeus (Athens's port) are the Cyclades. In this group is the famous volcanic island of Santorini (Thera), whose caldera (crater) still reminds us of the violent and catastrophic eruption that took place there more than 3,000 years ago. The Cyclades, occupying the main water route between Greece and Asia Minor, were among the first Aegean islands to be inhabited. Continuing southward from Cyclades is Crete, the eastern Mediterranean's largest island, standing alone in the sea and reminding everyone of the boundaries of the Greek cultural sphere.

Continuing eastward from the Cyclades, one encounters the Dodecanese island group. Geographically, the islands are in immediate proximity to Turkey and Asia, but culturally they are Greek. At one point in history, the largest island in the group, Rhodes, was the headquarters of the Knights of St. John, who fled Palestine in the aftermath of the Crusades and settled there. Later, the Turks kept control of this easternmost island in Greece. During their long occupation, they tried unsuccessfully to destroy Greek culture and replace it with their own.

Traveling north, almost all islands from Rhodes into the North Aegean and up to Thrace's coast are under Greek possession. Some are located just a few miles from the Turkish coast, and the majority of them were incorporated into Greece during the 1940s. The proximity of Turkey's coast allows for first-rate exploration into different lifestyles. Breakfast in a Greek coffee shop in Europe can be followed by a Turkish dinner in Asia after a short ferry ride. What a magnificent cultural experience! The northern Aegean Sea has fewer islands, but they are equally intriguing, especially Sporades and the large island of Evvia. The former has a long heritage and tourism tradition, whereas the latter is known for its unrefined beauty, left relatively undisturbed by the modern age of tourism.

Finally, often forgotten is the Ionian group of several islands located off Greece's western coast. Especially well known is Corfu, a first stop on the ferry voyage from Greece to Italy and vice versa. In this respect, it is as important today as it was during ancient times when the Ionian Islands served as bases for the Greek colonial expansion through the Mediterranean. One of these islands, Ithaca, was home to the legendary Odysseus. According to the Homeric legend, Odysseus participated in the war against Troy, after which he spent ten years on a seaborne odyssey en route to his home.

CHAPTER

8

Greece
Looks Ahead

Greece is a fascinating country. It offers a unique blend of tradition and modernity, conservativism and liberalism, Europe and Asia. In this final chapter, we will make an attempt to see what the future holds for Greece and its people.

Politically, the hardships of past times, when the country was governed by dictators or the military, appear to have come to an end. Internally, Greece is prepared to face the challenges of the twenty-first century. Externally, however, a number of political issues involving neighboring countries, particularly Turkey, remain unresolved. With Turkey's desire for membership in the European Union, these challenges will need to be met soon. In reality, many of these issues, such as a politically divided Cyprus, exist because of the longstanding mistrust between Greeks and Turks.

Traditions change slowly in this part of the world. To achieve the status of a highly developed country, Greece will have to transform its cultural system. Too many people expect the government to support them in a cradle-to-grave welfare system. Although the welfare state is an important part of European political tradition, it imposes a tremendous economic burden on the country and its people. In order to provide welfare, the government must collect more taxes. Eventually, the tax burden can limit economic growth and cause a perilous rise in unemployment.

Future socioeconomic changes must focus on adjusting unequal employment rates. The current gender imbalance is counterproductive: Female unemployment rates are twice that of Greek males. Working at the same jobs, women also earn much lower salaries than their male counterparts. This imbalance results from a slowly changing cultural system in which a male-dominated society is not willing to accept the fact that times are changing: Women are as capable as men in many areas. They deserve equal compensation for equal work, and they should be entitled to choose their own life professions. In rural areas, women are still expected to engage only in traditional female professions, or to dedicate themselves exclusively to being wives and mothers.

Rural areas are not transforming rapidly enough. In the future, wealth and power must be spread throughout urban and rural areas. The country can no longer allow the major urban centers, Athens and Thessaloniki, to develop at their expense. The countryside, although beautiful and inviting, requires serious attention. Greece cannot afford to allow its rural peoples and environments to languish as living museums of times past. Future projects designed to revitalize rural Greece should emphasize its two most important potentials: agriculture and tourism. Both activities can be highly competitive; Greece simply has to further develop its potential and find ways to promote them in today's world. Unfortunately, many rural people, because of their folk culture, strongly resist change. It may be difficult, for example, to introduce and implement the latest technologies of organic agriculture. Even though it would be far more profitable than traditional agriculture, changes in farming practices would require doing things differently in the context of a deeply entrenched lifestyle.

Elements of a traditional lifestyle are rapidly vanishing in Athens, where popular culture dominates. Cultural diffusion from the West has affected Greece's capital city, and it dominates the country's economy. Its citizens enjoy new technologies and economic practices, and the service sector has been greatly expanded. Because of this rapid expansion, however, Athens will face difficulties common to many other metropolitan centers. Pollution and traffic problems, in particular, are a price that must be paid. In order to prevent pollution, which ranks among Europe's worst, Athens will need to implement stringent environmental regulations. More high-speed highways will provide better and faster intra- and intercity connections. In order to revitalize the countryside and bring Athens some population relief, the government will have to improve living conditions in and accessibility to rural areas.

Demographic issues are becoming increasingly alarming throughout aging Europe. Greece, no doubt, will follow the rest of Europe with a declining birthrate, resulting in an aging and ultimately shrinking population. If, indeed, this occurs, the only option is for the country to open its doors to immigration. This poses a serious political and potential social problem, however, in a country that is 98 percent ethnically homogeneous. Few immigrants share Greek ethnicity; rather, they come from Africa, Asia, or neighboring Albania.

Immigrants are willing to take jobs that are less desirable and pay less. They also tend to reside in neighborhoods surrounded with others of their race and ethnicity. How an increase in immigration and the creation of such neighbor-hoods will affect Greece politically, economically, and socially is anyone's guess. The only certainty is that under existing demographic conditions, changes will undoubtedly occur in the foreseeable future.

Children wave Greek flags in anticipation of the arrival of the Olympic torch, shortly before the opening of the Athens Olympics in August 2004. Like many European countries, Greece's low birthrate and aging population have led to minimal population growth, which ultimately may force Greece to open its doors to immigrants to fill available jobs.

A growing population (even if by migration) means a larger labor force for the growing economy. Assuming social issues can be resolved, the positive impact of immigration will be continued economic growth. Despite its many regulations, integration into the European Union will continue to stimulate economic growth in Greece. With future EU expansion eastward, Greece will be in a splendid position to further benefit economically. If Turkey is accepted into the Union, it will add 70 million consumers to the common European market. This will be beneficial to many Greek companies and perhaps will also help improve relations between the two countries. Establishing a good economic relationship is a gigantic step toward ensuring a successful political relationship. The primary economic challenge in the near future is for Greece to balance its budget. Past governments have borrowed much more than they earned. A budget deficit burdens a nation's economy and can lead toward potential crisis and destabilization.

One of the best ways to fulfill budget obligations is through income from tourism. Greece's tourism has increased steadily during recent decades. With properly managed expansion of the tourist sector, the country can easily become one of the world's leading tourist destinations. It offers unmatched natural and cultural landscapes. A marvelous heritage, spectacular islands and seascapes, and rugged terrain can attract tourists. So, too, can sharply contrasting folk and popular cultures, quaint rural villages, and a world-class capital city. These, plus wonderful cuisine only add to the country's tourist-luring potential. On the other hand, Greece is on a long trip between the past and the future. Today, the country is at a crossroads. It can continue its journey into a modern and prosperous future, or turn back to the obscurity of the European periphery. It will be interesting to see which route Greece follows.

Facts at a Glance

Physical Geography

Country name	Long form: Hellenic Republic; Short form: Greece
Capital city	Athens
Location	Southeastern Europe; the southernmost country on the Balkan Peninsula. Shares boundaries with four European countries: Albania, 175 miles (282 kilometers); Bulgaria, 306 miles (494 kilometers); Turkey, 128 miles (206 kilometers); Macedonia, 152 miles (246 kilometers). Total borders with other countries: 763 miles (1,228 kilometers). Coastal boundaries: 8,497 miles (13,676 kilometers)
Area	Total: 51,146 square miles (131,468 square kilometers)
Climate and ecosystem	Mediterranean: hot, dry summers; mild, wet winters
Terrain	Mountainous interior with coastal plains; 2,000-plus islands
Elevation extremes	Mount Olympus reaches 9,570 feet (2,917 meters); the lowest elevation is sea level

People

Population	10,668,354 (July 2005 est.); males, 5,237,413 (July 2005 est.); females, 5,430,941 (July 2005 est.)
Population Density	80 per square kilometer
Population Growth Rate	0.19%
Net Migration Rate	2.34 migrant(s)/1,000 population (2005 est.)
Fertility Rate	1.33 children born/woman (2005 est.)
Life expectancy at birth	Total population: 79 years; male, 77 years; female, 82 years (2005 est.)
Median Age	40.5 years
Ethnic groups	Greeks 98%, others 2% (Turks, Albanians, Macedonians)
Religions	Greek Orthodox, 98%; Islam, 1.3%; other, 0.7%
Language	Greek 99%
Literacy	(age 15 and over can read and write) Total population, 97.5%; males, 98.6%; females, 96.5% (2003 est.)

Economy

Land Use	Arable land, 21.1%; permanent crops, 8.78%; other, 70.12%

Irrigated Land	5,490 sq. miles (14,220 sq. km) (1998 est.)
Natural Hazards	Earthquakes, volcanoes
Environmental Issues	Air pollution; water pollution
Currency	Euro
GDP (purchasing power parity) PPP	$242.8 billion (2005 est.)
GDP per capita (PPP)	$22,800 (2005 est.)
Labor Force	4.72 million (2005 est.)
Unemployment	10.8%
Labor force by occupation	68% services, 20% industry, 12% agriculture
Industries	Tourism, food and tobacco processing, textiles, chemicals, metal products, mining, petroleum
Leading trade partners	*Exports:* Germany, 13.1%; Italy, 10.3%; UK, 7.5%; Bulgaria, 6.3%; U.S., 5.3%; Cyprus, 4.6%; Turkey, 4.5%; France, 4.2% (2004)
	Imports: Germany, 13.3%; Italy, 12.8%; France, 6.4%; Netherlands, 5.5%; Russia, 5.5%; U.S., 4.4%; UK, 4.2%; South Korea, 4.1% (2004)
Exports	$18.54 billion (2005 est.)
Export Commodities	Manufactured goods, food and beverages, petroleum products, cement, chemicals
Imports	$48.2 billion (2005 est.)
Import Commodities	Basic manufactures, food and animals, crude oil, chemicals, machinery, transport equipment
Transportation	*Highways:* 72,700 miles (117,000 kilometers); 66,738 miles (107,406 kilometers) paved; *Railroads:* 1,597 miles (2,571 kilometers); 474 miles (764 kilometers) electrified; *Waterways:* 3.72 miles (6 kilometers) of Corinth Canal; *Airports:* 80

Government

Type of government	Republican parliamentary democracy
Head of State	Prime Minister Kostas Karamanlis
Independence	1829, from the Ottoman Empire
Administrative divisions	51 prefectures and 1 autonomous region
Communications	*TV stations:* 36 (1995); *Phones (including cellular):* 14,141,300 (2003); *Internet users:* 1,718,400 (2003)

6,000–4,000 B.C.	Evidence found of a significant presence of population in present-day Greece.
2,000–1,500 B.C.	Minoan civilization on Crete is at its zenith.
1,000–900 B.C.	Most recent wave of migration of Greek peoples.
776 B.C.	First Olympic Games are held.
700–500 B.C.	Mediterranean cultural realm is colonized extensively during this period.
667 B.C.	Colonists from Megara establish Byzantium, a colony on Bosporus that later becomes Constantinople.
Fifth century to fourth century B.C.	Greece wages victorious wars against Persians; Athens rises to power.
Third century B.C.	Alexander the Great makes Greece part of his Macedonian Empire.
Second century B.C. to fifteenth century A.D.	Greece is a part of Roman (later Eastern Roman) Empire.
330 A.D.	Constantine I moves capital of the Roman Empire to Constantinople.
1054	After the Great Schism, Greece is integrated into the Eastern Orthodox world.
1453–1821	Fall of Constantinople in 1453 marks the beginning of the Ottoman Empire's nearly 400-year occupation of Greece.
1829	Greece becomes independent from the Ottoman Empire.
1896	First modern Olympic Games begin in Athens.
1912	First Balkan War is waged against the Ottoman Empire.
1913	Second Balkan War is waged against Bulgaria.
1914	Greece enters World War I.
1918–1922	Greece enters conflict with the Turks.
1923	Treaty of Lausanne serves as basis for territorial exchange, as well as forced migrations of Greeks from Turkey and Turks from Greece.
1939–1945	Greece is involved in World War II.
1946–1950	Royalist and Communist factions in Greece wage a civil war; the Communists lose.

1952	Greece joins North Atlantic Treaty Organization (NATO).
1967	Greek military organizes a coup to overthrow the government.
1967–1974	The country is led by military junta.
1980	The Panhellenic Socialist Movement (PASOK) wins elections and holds power for most of 1980s and 1990s.
1981	Greece joins the European Economic Community, which is later renamed the European Union.
2001	Greece enters Eurozone; the euro replaces drachma as official currency.
2004	Summer Olympic Games held in Athens for second time.

Bibliography and Further Reading

Campbell, John Kennedy, and Philip Sherrard. *Modern Greece.* New York: Praeger, 1968.

Central Intelligence Agency. World Factbook: Greece. 2005. *http://www.odci.gov/cia/publications/factbook/geos/gr.html.*

Curtis, G.E., ed. *Greece: A Country Study.* Washington, D.C.: Library of Congress, 1994.

Dubin, Marc S. *The Greek Islands.* New York: DK Publishing, 1997.

Frankland, E. Gene. *Global Studies: Europe.* Guilford, CT: Dushkin/McGraw-Hill, 2002.

Harrington, Lyn. *Greece and the Greeks.* New York: Thomas Nelson and Sons, 1962.

Jordan-Bychkov, Terry G., and Bella Bychkova-Jordan. *The European Culture Area.* New York: Rowman and Littlefield, 2001.

National Statistical Service of Greece (NSSG). *Greece in Figures.* Pireas: NSSG, 2005.

Pavlović, Zoran. *Turkey.* Philadelphia: Chelsea House Publishers, 2004.

Stanislawski, Dan. "Dionysus Westward: Early Religion and the Economic Geography of Wine." *The Geographical Review,* 65, no. 4 (1975), 427–44.

Toynbee, Arnold J. *Greeks and Their Heritage.* New York: Oxford University Press, 1981.

Tozer, Henry Fanshawe. *Geography of Ancient Greece.* Chicago: Ares Publishers, 1974.

U.S. Department of State. *Background Notes.* 2005. *http://www.state.gov/r/pa/ei/bgn/3395.htm.*

Index

Index

page:

9:	New Millennium Images	53:	KRT/NMI
16:	© Lucidity Information Design	60:	New Millennium Images
18:	© Lucidity Information Design	64:	Gamma Presse/NMI
21:	New Millennium Images	69:	KRT/NMI
26:	BlackStar Photos/NMI	73:	Fayez Nureldine/AFP/ Getty Images/NMI
30:	New Millennium Images	79:	New Millennium Images
34:	New Millennium Images	83:	Zuma Press/NMI
37:	EPA/NMI	92:	AFP/NMI
43:	KRT/NMI		
49:	KRT/NMI		

Cover: New Millennium Images

ZORAN "ZOK" PAVLOVIĆ is a cultural geographer currently working at Oklahoma State University in Stillwater. *Greece* is Zok's seventh book authored or coauthored for the Chelsea House geography series MODERN WORLD NATIONS. He also authored *Europe* for the MODERN WORLD CULTURES series. Within the field of geography, his interests are culture theory, evolution of geographic thought, and geography of viticulture. When not writing, Zok enjoys gourmet cooking and long-distance motorcycle travel. He was born and raised in southeastern Europe.

CHARLES F. "FRITZ" GRITZNER is Distinguished Professor of Geography at South Dakota State University in Brookings. He is now in his fifth decade of college teaching, scholarly research, and writing. In addition to teaching, he enjoys traveling, writing, working with teachers, and sharing his love of geography with students and readers alike. As Consulting Editor and frequent author for the Chelsea House MODERN WORLD NATIONS and MODERN WORLD CULTURES series, he has a wonderful opportunity to combine each of these "hobbies."

Professionally, Gritzner has served as both president and executive director of the National Council for Geographic Education. He has received numerous awards in recognition of his academic and teaching achievements, including the National Council for Geographic Education's George J. Miller Award for Distinguished Service to geography and geographic education.